MOVE YOUR Æ

Know, Grow, and Show
Your Career Value

PAUL CARNEY

Published by Ishtot, Inc., Gulf Breeze, FL, U.S.A.
For information regarding bulk purchases, visit us at
www.PaulCarneyWorks.com

Cover design by: Brian Montes
Edited by: Proper Publishing, LLC
                            www.ProperPublishing.info
                            theproperpublisher@yahoo.com

ISBN: 978-1-984-30202-1 (trade paperback)

DEDICATION

I dedicate this book to Lisa; my best friend, business partner, vacation buddy, and wife. I would not have the success I enjoy today without her unwavering love and support as I explore the ideas to help people and build products, services and companies based on my dreams.

Kelly,

Keep you in high gear!

Paul Cary

CONTENTS

MOVE YOUR Æ

Introduction

In the first line of the introduction, I reveal my single intention of writing this book for you:

> To earn just enough of your trust to guide you
> to know, grow, and show your career value

Yes, it is that simple.

As I gathered information for industry conference speeches and spoke to people like you throughout the past few years, I realized how many of us share a common bond about our current career situation. We have been doing what we believe are the right things, following a prescribed path, keeping our heads down and doing our work on the way to a successful career and comfortable transition into retirement. Then one day, we looked up and found ourselves either in a dead-end job or even worse, out of a job. What happened?

While we were busy being busy, the value of our education, skills, experiences and the other attributes that have defined our career has changed. We have altered the formulas used in calculating our value to an organization or a job marketplace by technology, process improvements, and a globally-connected workforce. These forces have been coming together to create massive potholes in your career pathway, and it is time that you pay more attention and take action to avoid falling into the career sinkholes.

Do you remember those puzzles where you see two very similar pictures and are to find the five differences between them? The psychology behind why the changes are difficult to detect stems from our need to filter out small details to remain focused on and complete tasks. If you focused on every sound, smell or touch around you right now, you would not be able to read this book.

This filtering is what has happened to you in your career. While focusing on the big picture of where you were going, small changes were happening around you, like changes in how you use technology and the skills that companies seek in job candidates. We often hear today that robots and other forms of Artificial Intelligence (AI) will take over our jobs. While they may take over some of the mundane and dangerous tasks that we do not want to do, they will more likely change the way that we accomplish our work. Which means that it is even more important for you to know the value you bring to a job so you and new technology can work together towards better business results.

Given these changes, it is understandable that you have lost track of the value of your career in the job marketplace. It used to be simple to describe when a worker would get a college degree, work for one or two companies in his career and retire with a pension. Your career now encompasses a mixture of attributes, including your many jobs, skills, degrees, certifications, experiences, talents, companies, bosses, teams, compensation rates, benefits, training, vendors, and clients.

In addition, organizations want to consider more as they decide to hire you, including your qualities such as personality, aptitude, attitude, EQ (emotional intelligence), IQ (intelligence quotient), and LQ (learnability quotient). It is not a bad situation for you, just different than it used to be, and I will help you get back on the path by learning how to know, grow and show your career value.

Knowing your career value is not just about getting paid what you think you are worth. It is understanding the many aspects of you that make up your total career, as listed in the previous paragraph, then learning how to manage those aspects of your job through growth that will provide maximum benefit. And beyond knowing and growing your career value, you have to actively promote your career value.

I have found in my experiences and discussions with friends and colleagues like you that this one aspect of a person's career creates the most anxiety. Most people are simply not good at knowing how to effectively promote their value, which often leaves them being under appreciated and under compensated. This book will help you learn techniques to earn recognition, compensation, and promotions.

I am not only an avid reader on this topic, but my career has taken some crazy turns, some of which I did not expect. I had control over my career path when I started my own business in the late 1990s. After selling my company's product line to a national retailer, I joined another startup company, which sold shortly after. But I also left one of the groups of which I am a stock owner because the CEO and I could not come to terms with how to move the company forward. That was a major shock to my career.

I had another incident where my career was going very well until I encountered a form of professional neglect by one of the worst bosses I had ever had. While giving me positive feedback during our regular meetings and high-performance ratings on my annual performance review, this individual was sharing with other leaders that I was not doing my job. Luckily, I had built trusting relationships with those other leaders who shared this information with me, so I was fully aware of my tenuous situation.

While I have had many successes in my career, I faced times when I had limited control and faced challenges that left me wondering where I had gone wrong, which is why I understand much of what you are feeling right now. These experiences prompted me to bring the contents of this book together to help you be successful, even when your career is not going where you planned.

I cover dozens of reliable sources and have discussions with many people to take a pulse on what is happening. I have included some of the more relevant references in my book and provided footnotes to give attribution to those sources. I realized, over time, that I could share with you the general pulse of what I was seeing and feeling and it would bring together the disparate pieces from various sources into one truism:

**You are feeling lost and overwhelmed
because you are being left behind in the job marketplace.**

I am going to help you take charge of your career and show you how to manage your career value for maximum benefit.

If you are reading the physical book, you need a writing instrument and a highlighter to use this book effectively, as there are some brief questions at the end of some chapters. If you are using an e-book reader, use its features to keep notes along the way. Show the book some love. It is meant to be a tool for you to increase your value, so do not let the book sit there, a passive partner in your learning experience. Engage this book by writing notes and dog-ear or bookmark the pages as I focus on helping you:

Know, Grow and Show Your Career Value!

Part 1

Know Your Career Value

1

What Is Happening To Your Career?

Success is how high you bounce when you hit bottom.

— General George Patton

Anxiety has you feeling overwhelmed and lost in your job or career. What happened? You had skills that were moving you forward but somewhere along the way those skills and experiences are not worth as much as you thought. And worse, it looks like those same skills are not going to help you stay employed unless you act fast.

You feel that you are on the skills treadmill - you have to keep learning and growing, yet what you learned yesterday is not helping you move ahead. Additionally, you feel overwhelmed by all of the options for education, training, and advice, experiencing paralysis[1], whereby instead of each additional piece of information providing help, it makes it worse.

Are you frustrated that you have worked hard to put yourself in a place where your job should provide a decent standard of living for you and your family, but it is not working out that way? Are you aggravated that no matter what you seem to do to get noticed, it is as if you are invisible?

If you have recently lost your job or are tired of your current situation and are looking for a job, you know that it has become challenging to find a new opportunity. Creating dozens of resume versions and applying to online jobs is not getting you any traction. Even if you can connect with friends and associates, you seem to be passed over for the job because someone else was "more qualified." What does that mean and how do you fix it?

Technology is creating rapid changes in how we work. The work you do today is not the same as it was yesterday. Along with the pressure to keep improving efficiencies, there are steep learning curves for the new processes and tools you must use. Previously, all you had to know was how to enter information into a machine and push the start button. If the device stopped working, you called in a "technician" who would diagnose and fix it.

Today, you have to know what happens when the machine stops working. What caused it to stop? What can you do to get it started again? When do you give up trying to solve the problem and ask for help? These are problem-solving skills that include the need for knowledge about how the entire system works so that you can diagnose the issue and fix it. But that was not how your teachers and bosses prepared you for the work environment. They merely helped you get trained in a skill and let you take it from there.

What happens after you hear that harmonious "ding" and that infamous "check-engine" light illuminates in your car?

There's anxiety, followed immediately by a knot in your stomach and the rock in your gut letting you know that something is wrong. There it is - that somewhat innocuous engine shape, or just the words "Check Engine" staring you in the face. Something bad just happened, and this is going to cost a lot of money.

Back in the day, it was simple and easy to see where everything was under the hood of the car. Today, if you look under the hood, it is a tangle of wires connecting every part of the vehicle to the other, and the computer is the one who tells me something is wrong, but not necessarily what is wrong and how to fix it. I have to take my car to a shop where they hook it up to yet another computer that spits out codes to the newly-trained technician, who interprets the information and prepares the plan of attack to fix it. Everyone today has to be more adept at using newer technically-oriented tools or risk being left behind, which leaves you less in control and not sure what do to next.

Your "Check-Career" light is illuminating

I will help you calibrate your career without costly trips to the shop.

Unemployment in the United States is at an all-time low, and the Bureau of Labor and Statistics (BLS) have reports that show a widening gap between the number of workers available and job openings. Workforce experts and government representatives at all levels attempt to explain this phenomenon as a "skills gap" in which the skills and experiences that companies need in their workers, the majority of applicants simply do not have the skillsets required. Many point to the obsolete curriculums in our high schools or colleges, while others lay blame at the feet of the workers saying that they are not doing enough to keep up with the changing needs of the workplace.

But it is more than just a skills gap. It is a "value gap" in which the skills that we have are no longer valued like they used to be. A college degree used to get you into a job that paid a living wage. The gap between the value of that degree and what you can earn with it in the job marketplace has changed in such a way, widening as the earning potential for the degree has remained steady or dropped while the debt burden of the degree has risen.

What are you to do? You need to understand better your career value, not only what it is today, but how you can stabilize and strengthen it so that you are not left behind. As I stated in the introduction to this book, my goal is to earn enough of your trust that you will know why it is so vital for you to take control of your career. If you leave it to others, like the government or the company for whom you work, you hand them the ability to direct where you land at the end of your career and when you will be able to retire. I strongly suspect that you don't want to do that.

When was the last time there were so many choices you didn't know what to do? It is a standard issue in business marketing when an organization offers too many options, which can stall the decision-making ability and cause the consumer not to make a purchase. Psychology professionals researched the concept of "satisficing[2]," which is how a person comes to a "good enough" rationalization to make a decision.

Nobel Laureate Herb Simon, Ph.D., first coined this term and described why you are better off choosing the first decent choice that fits your preference as opposed to exhaustively processing all options until you find the perfect one. Because we cannot efficiently gather all of the information needed to make a "maximized" decision, our brains are not equipped to process all of the information.

The rapid changes in technology and ever-expanding need to grow your skills puts you into a similar situation where you are required to develop stronger skills at filtering out what is not essential to your career and exclusively focusing on what you need to do to grow and promote your career value.

There is also a natural tendency of our brains, which have evolved, to manage fear and risks for us to survive[3]. You may know this as the "fight or flight" response that describes how you tend to act when faced with a situation that challenges your safety or security.

You have some degree of control over your limbic brain, which is the part of the brain responsible for this reaction, but it requires quite a bit of training to be able not immediately to react to a given situation. People whose jobs put them in stressful situations where the environment can change very quickly, like police, firefighters or fighter jet pilots, train extensively to recognize that they are in the "fight or flight" mode and manage the flood of hormones that course through their bodies during this acute stress response[4]. While your life may not be in danger, losing your job or getting caught in a dead-end career are enough to trigger your concerns about safety and wellbeing. This stress, along with the fact that the requirements of your job are becoming more complicated and complex, indicates that you need a way to create simplicity and reduce the ineffective stress to achieve your goals.

On the topic of your brain, you also face challenges with your natural cognitive and emotional tendencies when you are attempting to process information and make a decision.

Those biases can create obstacles in ways you do not recognize. For instance, as human beings, our mental operations of thinking and reasoning are deeply connected to how we solve problems and decide on a path.

As thinkers, we seek confirmation of what we regard, always looking for clues to support our beliefs. As reasoners, we aim to affirm and boost our ego to create a positive psyche through which our lives will flow. By the end of this book, you will have a better understanding of where you are using either of these tendencies.

There is a term that has been used to help organizations understand the variability that they face, and it applies to you, too. It is called "VUCA," which stands for Volatility, Uncertainty, Complexity, and Ambiguity. It was introduced by the U.S. Army War College[5]. See the chart on the following two pages to understand how each of these applies to your career.

	Meaning	**How it Applies to Your Career**
Volatility	- Tendency for something to change quickly, sometimes unexpectedly - Usually indicates an unfavorable change of events	- Change in boss - Company is acquired by another organization - Other team members are terminated for no apparent reason
Uncertainty	- There are doubts about a situation - Not sure what results will occur if you make a decision to take an action	- Unsure if the company has enough money for payroll - Two team members have done similar tasks but been treated differently - What you did last year, and was praised for, does not seem to be pleasing your boss now

	Meaning	**How it Applies to Your Career**
Complexity	- Intricate - Contains many interwoven parts or connections	- How your career journey has brought you to where you are today - An operational risk is exposed and involves people from multiple divisions to resolve - The political relationships of the many managers creates a minefield to avoid when discussing team issues
Ambiguity	- Vague, unclear - Words or terms can be interpreted in multiple ways	- Your boss has asked you to complete a project, but you do not know what results are needed - The president of the company asks everyone to "buckle down" and you don't know if that means to work harder or spend less money

In short, VUCA is a practical code for awareness and readiness[6], which helps describe why reading this book and following the lessons will help you build your awareness and develop a plan so that you are not left behind in the job marketplace.

Are you in a low-paying job, unable to see a way to improve your situation? Are you saving enough for retirement so that you can safely and comfortably rely on what you have saved instead of working to create an income stream? Or worse, you find that you have to work into your 70's because you cannot afford to give up that income?

You, like many others, have expressed frustration at times that you do not get recognized and rewarded for all of your hard work. Or when you do have great success, it just means that your boss piles more onto your workload. You lose trust when you don't feel you are being paid attention to or are not rewarded fairly for your contributions. Get that trust back by taking small, actionable steps to document and grow your career value.

If you have been in the job market lately looking for work, you will understand the fear, anxiety, and frustration that many people feel in trying to connect the dots from their value to a new role. One challenge in finding a new job, especially if you have a current position, is that you will keep the search secret from most of your colleagues because you don't want your boss or your company to discover you are looking for other opportunities.

While keeping your search quiet from your current company may be needed to avoid a sudden termination if they are not happy with your activity, it also severely limits your ability to get your message out to your network so that they can help. Using a social media site like Facebook or

LinkedIn to ask for ideas on what opportunities exist is a great way to learn about a job opening that is not widely known. You need to find the right balance to keep your current job while you search because keeping your current income while you look creates less anxiety than if you have no income at all. Most talent acquisition professionals recommend that you follow this rule if possible.

One of the most significant obstacles to searching for a new role is the fear of failure: what if you try to get a new job and are not selected? At least a few people are going to know that you are searching. That number can be even larger if you are not currently employed and use your online and offline networks. When people know you are looking or have interviewed a few times, they are going to follow up when they see you by asking about the status of your job search. You don't want to have to tell them that you didn't get the job, not only because you feel like a failure, but you also don't usually understand why you did not get the job.

It is not surprising that job candidates have lost trust in the recruiting process, given the way applicants are treated. You spend your time and money to prepare a resume that highlights some of your accomplishments and includes how you will help the company meet business goals. But does a resume really explain you, even if it is well written and includes a fabulous cover letter?

How do you know how to stand out if you are not able to see the candidates against whom you are competing? Given that you do not have this insight, you make educated guesses on how to state your value using action verbs and keywords. If your "keywords" on the resume are not what the recruiter or hiring manager wants, it doesn't matter what value you may think you have because you are not going to get past the initial screening, which a computer typically does today.

So you do your very best by applying, filling out the list of education and past jobs that you repeat with a mind-numbing efficiency across every company's application system, and you wait. And wait. And wait. If you are fortunate, you get the canned auto-reply email that tells you that they received your application and will be in touch with you if you meet the qualifications. Then, you wait. And wait. And wait. No more information is shared.

Perhaps, anywhere from 6 weeks to 6 months later, you get another automatically-generated email telling you that while they appreciate your efforts, they are selecting someone else and you are no longer being considered. But fear not, as they will keep your resume on file in case future openings are a fit. I can say emphatically that most companies do not go back and search that stack of applications. Why should they? When they post the next job, they will get hundreds, if not thousands of bright-eyed, eager applicants who think that they have a chance this time and the entire process plays out once again.

We don't accept this in other aspects of our lives. Look at what Dominos and Papa Johns have done with their pizza ordering and delivery systems. They show you a graphic with each step indicating when it happened or will happen, and by whom. You know precisely where your pizza is in the process. Or look at how you can use web-based tools to create your car, choosing everything from the color to the stereo system, then get regular updates on where your vehicle is in the manufacturing process and when it will be delivered to you.

If those organizations can show you all of that information for your new car and a pizza, why can't companies provide you with updates about where you are in the application process? It must be because they don't want you to see what is going on. The process of selecting people for a company is very inefficient.

Typically, systems are not connected or do not contain the ability to show you this information. Additionally, an organization will usually not want to show those that are not being considered until the process is complete and they have sent out acceptance offers. The same is true even if you were screened out at the very beginning of the application process.

I had a manager explain to me why she wanted to keep all options open and not notify the applicants who had been screened out due to lack of qualifications. She said that if she interviewed the five people on her final list of consideration, and none of them were good, she might then look at more people who were further down the list. I summarized her process to conclude that she lowers the bar of what will be accepted if the first interviews are duds.

She countered that the other people might have more than meets the eye on their resume, so she doesn't want to send them away since we spent the energy to find them in the first place.

And that sums up what is wrong with today's recruiting process:

1. We have a difficult time determining someone's value from just a resume, cover letter and what they filled out on their application.

2. Our recruiting processes are not efficient and do not take advantage of today's technologies, like the ones that allow us to track every step in the operations used to deliver a new car or pizza, to let the candidate see his status on an applicant dashboard on the company's website.

I do not have the answer to fix the recruiting process. Many professionals are working on ideas to come up with a better way. But I can say that while this process is broken, it is essential that you develop a way to know, grow and show your career value to stand out from the crowd. The ideas in this book are not an "all or nothing⁷" approach to your career, because that is not the goal. My goal is to help you navigate your way on your journey, taking incremental steps that will eventually add to your career. Keep reading, and I will show you how to do this.

Chapter Debrief

- While jobs are available, it has become more difficult to be noticed and selected
- Problem-solving skills are essential to develop
- Be aware of how VUCA (volatility, uncertainty, complexity, ambiguity) affects your career
- Developing persuasive resumes and making professional connections are required to find opportunities

Your Turn

1. What three skills are most important to your job today?

2. List two examples each for how Volatility and Uncertainty affected your job recently.

2

Take Control of Your Career

> Until you make the unconscious conscious, it
> will direct your life, and you will call it fate.
>
> — C.G. Jung

Your career value is not fate. You control the value and contribute to it as much or as little as you want, taking it as far as you demand of yourself.

Dr. Stephen Covey, a prolific author, and motivational leader, often stated that there are three constants in life:

- Change
- Choice
- Principles[8]

One of my favorite quotes of his regarding those three constants is:

I am not a product of my circumstances.
I am a product of my decisions.

In this statement, Dr. Covey helps you realize that even when situations you have limited control over cause you to land in a specific spot, the decisions you make, at that moment, determine the path of your career journey.

I say to you right now: No matter where you are in your career or how much you have invested so far, the decisions you make today and tomorrow will have a direct impact on where you go next. In short, I remind you that you can permit yourself to:

Take control of your career

To do this, you must take actionable steps, which is not hard. In fact, think of it as micro-actions; smalls steps that add up to big journeys. To get started, you need to develop the skills to make little things into habits. James Clear, an authoritative leader on how to discover habits and routines that make you the best you can be, wrote one of the best articles I have seen regarding habits. "The 3 R's of Habit Change[9]" states that behavioral psychology researchers have repeatedly shown how the following items will help you be more successful:

- Reminders
- Routines
- Rewards

And it all starts with small actions. You would not plan an entire wedding or large business conference in one day, why do you expect to build and grow your career in a similar fashion? You can break down the steps into one of those items above and develop a program that works best for you.

I add to his compelling message the chance for you to face each day by being thankful for something that makes you appreciate what you have accomplished. Perhaps it is a favorite song that you play, or a note that someone wrote to you, or a picture that reminds you of a great relationship. Whatever it is, be accountable to yourself by following my lead in helping you determine and increase your merit.

Jeff Bezos, Amazon CEO, describes succinctly that, "We all get to choose our life stories. It's our choices that define us, not our gifts.[10]" While we share similar degrees, certifications, experiences, and jobs with others, we are all unique in how we have accumulated our career stature. Do not try to duplicate the careers of other people, but copy the parts that add to your value. Use the inspiration you see in other people's jobs to go above and beyond, adding even more to your career caliber.

You are not going to do this by following the rules. I have not always followed the rules, and it has brought me success when I zigged while others were following the "zag" road sign. I recall the first time I shared this nugget of wisdom with my then 12-year-old daughter. The family was at the dinner table, with my daughter sitting to my left and my wife and son were directly across the square table from us. Dinner was finishing, and my daughter was upset with a situation at school with a teacher. I do not remember the exact details of the injustice that occurred, but it had to do with the students having to follow a rule that my daughter and her friends did not agree was necessary. I do remember that it was not an issue of student safety, but more about acceptable behavior during the school day.

At this point, I looked directly at her and said, "You know, you do not have to follow a rule if you do not want to." My daughter's eyes lit up as she said the longest rendition of the word "really" that I have ever heard. Of course, at this point, I felt the look from my wife from across the table as she said, "Don't tell her that!" "But it's true," I said. Then I finished the rest of the story. "You do not have to follow a rule, as long as you are willing to accept the consequences."

And that is the same message to you. I recommend that when it comes to your career today, you have to be willing to bend the rules to your will, as both time and technology are going to push you around if you let them. Add on your boss's need for performance improvements and your company's desire for efficiencies, and you now understand why you feel the pressure and why it is up to you to take charge.

You (and your colleagues) are most likely the company's largest expense, so if they can automate your job with a cheaper substitution, they will. An organization's purpose, whether a for-profit or non-profit entity, is to turn inputs (resources like money, people, time) into outputs (goods, services). In managing expenses, they will strive to minimize the costs needed to create the output, and if you are one of their most significant costs, it is not surprising that you feel the squeeze. Simply put, you have to provide more value than an algorithm, or some automation will replace you.

Are you getting paid your value?

That is a big question, and I am going to guess I know your answer, but let's look at three possible ones:

Yes

Congratulations! But that does not mean you are off the hook. Rapid changes in technology and expectations at work mean that you must continue to learn and grow. As you finish this book, you will learn how you can do that effectively.

Maybe? I do not know?

That's okay. You are probably in the same boat as many of the other readers. When did someone ever teach you what your career value is? What tools did they use? How did they take all of the unique combinations of skills, experiences and so many other attributes of you and create a value to represent them? No one has done this for you, and that is why when asked the question, you do not have a precise answer.

No

After you look around and see that more than half of the readers have their hands up, you can put your hand down. I know, it is tough. You do so much for your team, your boss, your employer, but it just does not feel that you are getting the right value from it. Perhaps there is a lack of training or minimal learning opportunities presented to you. It could be that your boss does not display the skills and abilities to lead the team successfully. Or it could simply be that the company, in its efforts to minimize expenses (of which you are a large part) and maximize profits (by extracting more effort out of you), you are not getting paid what you are worth. It's time for you to take control and not only define your career value, but make your case by promoting your value so that you CAN earn what you are worth.

The largest issue you face is not that your job will be eliminated tomorrow. It is only true for manual labor jobs for which a repeatable, repetitive algorithm can be designed in which a robot can do the tasks. For everyone else, the challenge is that your job will continuously change over time and if you are not aware of the change and respond to it, one day you will suddenly find yourself no longer able to do the job and on the street looking for your next role. Don't let that happen to you. I am going to show you how to take control.

Hard work is not enough anymore. It will get you on a path, but unless you focus on the right opportunities, you may end up on a dead-end street. You have to re-prove yourself over and over. At the same time, you have to continuously promote your value, which is your unique mix of skills, talents, experiences, education and a myriad of other attributes. This form of self-promotion is difficult and leaves you without an easy process to qualify and quantify your career value.

How do you fix this? Most people tell you to have a plan. While that is where you want to end up, there are a few small steps you can take in preparation for your grand plan. Planning is not easy, but if you follow the path I lay out for you, I will walk you to your plan. Before you set up and activate your plan, you have to understand why it is essential to be able to determine your value and promote that value in the open marketplace. You have to be able to track and manage your value, which is something you were not taught in school nor something that your employer provides for you. In fact, most employers do not tout your value, because either that means that they will have to pay you more or they will lose you to the competition.

That is why your value belongs to you, and you are the one who is uniquely qualified to track it, grow it and sell it. Once you follow my steps, you will know how to set up the plan that will take you down the road for which you have been looking. Even more, you will put yourself in a position to earn what you are worth by being able to describe and provide your value succinctly.

I have been working for over 30 years and have the notches in my head to prove the hard knocks. In the latter part of my career, I joined a large organization. I started in the technical group, using my background and experiences to lead software projects. That was going well until I realized that to progress on the leadership career ladder at this organization, I had to move to another business unit. The technology group at our operations center was not going to offer leadership roles in the technology group for quite a few years.

I applied for and proved my value to move into Human Resources. I know, I get asked the question a lot: How in the world can you move from IT to HR? Well, I have a unique mix of teaching, business, technology, and leadership qualities. I also have the agility to take what I have learned in those many areas and apply them to new situations. Flexibility not only earned me a place on the leadership track, but I earned promotions with more levels of responsibility. At one point, I was managing nine different HR teams in our operations center, including Talent Acquisition, Employee Relations, Employee Communications, Employee Perks and Programs, Multimedia Services, Employee Service Center, HR Analytics, Payroll, and the Learning Management System.

Then, I achieved a goal two years earlier than expected: I was selected to join the elite "Executive Development Program." It is a 2-year, intensive program where a cohort of leaders work together on projects and are introduced to all areas of the organization while participating in multiple advanced leadership training sessions onsite at one of the nation's best graduate schools of business. That program was not a crown jewel to cap my career, but instead was one more opportunity along my continuing career path to learn and grow, of which I took complete advantage.

And then it happened: I ran smack up against a boss that didn't value my skills. At first, I could not understand what was happening, as I have consistently been aware of my talents and abilities, working hard to get myself into roles where I can be the transformational leader that I had proven to be multiple times before. The team had a strategic plan, with which the leader agreed, and we were not only meeting the goals of the plan but were flexible to meet the unexpected demands that came up during the years. But no matter what I did, it was not right, and when I asked what I needed to do, I received no constructive feedback.

That was the first moment in my career where I did not have the answers, even more so than when I launched an online baby basket business in 1997, the early days of the World Wide Web. I had heard stories about bad bosses, and I had a few that were not the best, but all provided me with feedback to some degree. Even worse, this boss was sharing things about me to other leaders, topics which were not shared with me, which caused a loss of trust in my leader.

I sought advice from other tenured employees, including senior leaders who were mentors to me. Like other times in my career, I have employees who followed me from team to team. In my career, that also occurred from company to company. As I talked with more people, I came across the crux of the issue: my boss did not value me the same way others did. It was that simple. While others could see how my knowledge, experience, skills, talents, personality, leadership abilities and so much more provided a lot of value to the company, this person did not assign the same value. No matter how much you have done and accomplished, if the other party does not assign any value to it, there is a definite lacking.

As I began to come to this new realization of the value gap that exists when someone does not appreciate your career value, I found that others were having the same issue. So many had career anxiety because they were not being valued any longer, either. That is what brought me to the point of pulling the data together and developing a solution to the issue of qualifying and quantifying your value in a transparent way so it can be viewed and used to objectively determine the best opportunities for you to apply your value and drive business results. I am sharing this information so you can learn how to manage and promote your value to move ahead in your career.

It is difficult to argue with success, but it is a long and continuous race to achieve it. Be prepared to document your value as you create it. It is tough to remember all of the great things that you do, so you must develop a habit of writing down notes. They don't have to be extensive or complex, just a few words or phrases. Contrary to what your 4th-grade writing teacher drilled into you, complete sentences are not required.

Having a plan is not the complete answer. In fact, it usually gets in the way of completing tasks because it becomes a burden, and causes anxiety. Having a vision or dream of where you want to go is the best way to be successful. I know because I have lived it. You can work backwards from that vision to some point close to today to see a possible map of how you are going to get there.

There have been many times in my life where I have "projected" what I want it to be like when I reach a goal. And guess what - it worked! Not every time, but it worked enough that it became second nature to me. I remember the first time I expressed this to my wife. She thought I was crazier than my normal crazy. But as I explained it to her, she began to understand why I do it. It helps me see the path and make sure I am staying on it. It also allows me to be flexible as opportunities arise. As long as the result will get me close to where I want to end up in my vision, it pays to zig and zag.

My goal is to show you how to set a vision of your career value, both what it is now and what it can be in the future. To do this, you will need to follow a few steps as I guide you through them. As I stated in the introduction to this book, if you are reading the paperback version of the book, have a writing instrument (pencil, pen, crayon) and a highlighter ready. In fact, I strongly recommend that you go out and buy a box of new crayons and use your favorite color.

Why would you do this? Because it is a little different, even irreverent. Do you remember that smell when you first opened the new box of crayons? The crayons are staring at you with perfectly-pointed tips, which you know you will never get them back to that point once you start caressing the page to create your masterpiece.

Why not treat yourself to a little piece of your childhood as we begin your journey. Every time you pick up that crayon to jot an idea in the book or answer the questions at the end of each section, you will remember that you are unique and that is a good feeling, one you should embrace. In fact, be sure to take images of the "Your Turn" section at the end of the chapters and share them with me on social media so we can all enjoy your success.

Okay - buy the crayons. I will be right here when you get back.

Chapter Debrief

-   Decisions you make directly affect your outcome
-   Use the "3 R's of Habits:" Reminders, Routines, Rewards
-   Provide more value than an algorithm, or some automation will replace you

Your Turn

1. Name one person who you admire and two attributes about him/her that you can copy.

2. Pick one activity from work that you want to change, then create at least one Reminder, one Routine, and one Reward.

3

Finding Your Balance

People with goals succeed because they know where they're going.

— Earl Nightingale

With all that is happening in your career, you need to develop self-awareness to avoid burnout and find ways to reduce your stress. Finding that balance puts the odds back in your favor as your career continues to grow in order to provide for your current living standard and to secure a solid one for tomorrow.

Working with other leaders through the years, I witnessed how many of them let one aspect of their life, typically their job, take over and have a devastating impact on their families and friends. After learning from their mistakes, I established a set of priorities that help maintain balance in my life.

While the demands of my career and personal life will change from time to time, it must come back to a balancing point, or I lose focus on what is essential. For me, those priorities are:

1. **Me**

   If I do not take care of myself over the long term, then I cannot be helpful to others. I need the strength to handle all of the challenges I face, and if I am not focused on my own needs once in a while, I lose that durability.

2. **My Family and Close Friends**

   This group is next on my priority list because they are the ones who are with me in all chapters of my life, offering the support and love that helps me be successful.

3. **My Community**

   Again, this is the group of people connected across the many aspects of my life. They are the other parents that help us raise our children, the teachers, police, neighbors, business owners and churchgoers who make up the community in which I live.

4. **My Job**

   While this may jump to the top once in a while, it cannot remain there if I am going to remain a healthy, balanced person.

It is that last item in the list that causes many people to go astray when they let it rise above many, if not all, of those other priorities and let it stay there. It has become harder for you to rebalance the job priority, given that the rapid changes and process improvements in your work require you to expend more efforts just to keep up. I am going to help you manage that process so that you can increase your career value and bring the list of priorities back in balance.

———

Are you prepared today if you lost your job tomorrow? You have to keep up with change, or it will leave you behind. Your company is focused on process improvements and efficiencies, which make your job even harder since you have to do your regular work and allocate time to determine what is broken and how it can be fixed, then implement it.

Your boss talks with you about your performance, hopefully, more than once a year, as the company aims to squeeze more work out of you without having to hire more people. If you are fortunate, you might get a little more money. Either way, it creates more stress on you to perform more with less.

Beyond your need to provide a secure living for you and your family, you have goals and desires to be successful at your job. Among those wants are:

- Development
- Achievement
- Advancement
- Impact
- Purpose
- Respect
- Acknowledgment of your Achievements
- Recognition and Rewards for your Value

You have to combine focus with recharge by creating cycles of high performance with down times. Athletes, from high school to professional sports, follow athletic conditioning cycles of intense workout followed by rest for their muscles to hit peak development. You have to do the same with your career by creating bursts of learning that you manage and track, followed by periods of rest. Unfortunately, your boss and company want you to have your foot on the gas pedal the entire time without any break. It would be like if you took a performance race car for a ride and took it up to the red line of RPMs and kept it there for hours. Eventually, that engine is going to burn up, similar to how you will burn out if you do not find a way to manage your career value.

Job loss or a significant change in your job situation can strike at any time. What have you done to prepare for this? Do you know the value you have added to your team and organization well enough so that you can succinctly describe it to someone to get a new job? I do not mean that you can write it down on a resume, although that is also difficult for most people to do effectively, to be able to describe, using stories, how you added value by analyzing a situation, preparing a plan and solving problems. That is what your next boss is going to be looking for during any conversation about a new job opportunity. The time to work on knowing and describing your value is NOW so that you have control over the situation when you need it most.

Do you search for purpose? I am sorry to say, but you have more than one purpose. Your entire life is filled with many reasons for you to accomplish goals, help people and even get up each day. Don't just focus on one big purpose, but look at the many values you add. Like a career, you build your goal over time, not just reach it one day. And to develop your job, you must be learning and growing, finding a sense of purpose in the work you do, which changes over time, and that is okay. I will help you map and document your career value to help you understand and promote your career purposes in life.

You want a career where you feel good about your contributions. Unlike the past, this is not necessarily with just one company. It might be comfortable to stay with one organization, but you will limit your opportunities to grow.

You may continue to increase the value you add to the group by knowing the culture, processes, and people, but over the long term, your value will diminish because it is not readily transferable to other organizations or jobs. I am not saying that you should avoid staying with a company for most of your career, but that you should be aware of the effect this has on your value in the overall marketplace.

Since your career will not only span jobs and companies but most likely professions, your ability to document and show your value is essential to your career success. And you were not taught what you need to survive in your career. While your teachers and professors may have imparted some knowledge to you, did they help you understand what you need to do in the workplace to be successful? Did they teach you the "soft skills" you need on how to navigate company politics or handle disappointment when you don't reach a goal? As you are realizing, contrary to a popular book, you did not learn everything you needed to learn when you were in Kindergarten.

How do you manage risk? Are you prepared if a significant event occurs that directly affects your job, such as the closing of your company, sale of your business to another one or worse, you are let go for any reason? You may not have given it much thought, or perhaps you simply do not want to think about it because it makes you feel uncomfortable.

While it is not the most pleasant of thoughts, you need to be aware of the risk you face if you lose your job. If you don't plan and anticipate, you are forced to react. You do not want to put yourself in a position where you have to quickly respond because, under those circumstances, you face more challenges because you have:

- Less control
- Higher anxiety
- Limited visibility for future outcomes

If you instead plan and anticipate, you take a pro-active stance while you have the security of your current job. By planning, you have:

- Stronger ability to view opportunities and choose the ones you want
- More control to manage the pace at which you learn and grow
- Better visibility of the path that will help you achieve your goals

Many times in my life people learn about my achievements and say that I am "lucky." That's a funny word: luck. It implies that success or achievement came about through a random set of activities rather than as a direct result of a concerted set of planned events. "Good fortune" and "chance happenings" are more traditional ways of saying it, and they push forward the idea that I did not have much to do with the results.

What most people don't understand is that many times the results occur because of hard work, determination, and the perseverance to keep going. There are also many failures behind success. While being in the "right place at the right time" does have a touch of chance included, it is more about pro-actively putting yourself in situations where you can see and take advantage of the opportunities when they arrive.

When I sold my Capango database system to South49 Solutions in 2005, that was a direct result of meeting the owner of South49 Solutions at a networking event in

Northern Virginia. I remember the night very well. There was a networking event at the offices of an organization called CIT in Herndon. It was after work and back in the late 1990s and early 2000s, there was a lot of entrepreneurial activity in the greater Washington, D.C., area, which meant that many activities were going on. That week, I had already attended an event. As the time arrived for me to leave work, I was tired. I had a long day, focused on a new project. I also knew that traffic would be busier if I went that way instead of my usual route home. When you live in the Washington, D.C. area as I did for 15 years, traffic is a significant part of your life.

As I got to my vehicle, I decided I was going to go home instead. I had met some new people at the previous event; I was tired and ready to get home. I was taking the traffic path of least resistance. I don't remember exactly why, but as I started driving, I gave myself a pep talk and changed my mind. I am going to stop by, say hi to the few people who I knew were going to be there, and then leave. What I didn't realize, is that is the night I met the owner of South49 Solutions. We talked about our respective businesses and were interested in learning more about each other. His company was moving into new office space in a week, so I set up a time to visit and bring lunch. From that one night, I sold the Capango system to South49 Solutions, became a co-owner of the company, and helped to create the incredibly successful Natural Insight system from the Capango platform. That result was not luck, but a direct result of putting myself in a situation to have the door of opportunity available for me to open. And you need to do that, too.

Jeff Bezos, Amazon CEO, likes the phrase "work-life harmony," as "work-life balance" indicates that there is a strict trade-off[11]. Many writers and media hosts have suggested that Millennials want more flexibility in their jobs so that they can accomplish the work-life harmony. Well, I can tell you as a GenXer, that many of my fellow GenX colleagues and just as many Boomers want that same flexibility and work-life harmony. It is not generation specific. And since so many of us want that flexibility between our work and non-work lives, it is more important for us to be able to have a clear description of our career value outside of the framework of our current company and job so that it is portable. The more loosely-coupled our career value is to our current situation, the more easily we can use that value to open new opportunities, whether it is to get more flexibility, more money or just a chance to continue learning and growing. Having that portable value is key to making this happen.

From the time you started school, you were a number tossed into a calculation. Typically, those numbers were added together and averaged, like assigning grades or taking standardized tests so that the administrators could determine a "norm" by which your development is measured. The Human Resources team in your organization is no different. They use your information, from performance reviews to pay, to determine where you are relative to others on your team or in your company.

Do you want to be the average of a bunch of statistics captured about you by a Human Resources system or do you want to tell the world about the complete you? From the use of decision matrices when you are considered for a new job to determining your pay increase from the overall pool of available money, your information is being used to make decisions that directly affect you. While they are playing the numbers games, it is up to you to learn what rules they create to understand what it takes to be at the top. Now you have an opportunity to learn from this book and stack the deck in your favor.

The IoT (Internet of Things) is a network in which each device at a node is a "dumb" item, with little value but to collect a piece of data and pass it along. In some cases, nodes exist simply to pass something from one point to the next without even collecting data or understanding what it is passing. You don't want to be one of these nodes. You want to be adding value to everything that you do through documentation so that others recognize it and the marketplace rewards for it.

You, like so many others, desire to be proud of the work you do. Think about the last time that you left your job and felt proud because you accomplished something. Didn't that feel great? It may have been hard work and you were exhausted when you left, but you had a deep feeling of satisfaction in your body. Do you need to love the work that you do? It is great if you can get to that point, but not necessary.

What you need is to have a level of satisfaction that keeps you going. It is that pride and satisfaction that allows you to face the next day with a more optimistic attitude. Managing your anxiety, along with finding purpose and using the lighter side of life, have shown that your positive approach can help you achieve success[12].

Preparation is key. You typically plan for a vacation, get-togethers with family and friends, and the development of your relationships. Your career is no different. It requires some preparation, but it does not have to be overwhelming. You can develop incremental steps that will guide you down a path, and this book will help you get started.

Chapter Debrief

- Understanding and describing your priorities is an important step in your career

- Use career strength training and conditioning cycles, with bursts of learning followed by periods of use, for best results

- Pro-actively putting yourself in situations where you can see and take advantage of the opportunities when they arrive

Your Turn

1. Create your personal list of priorities and use two phrases to describe each item in the list.

2. Recall one time in the past 30 days where you gave yourself a pep talk and describe two reasons why it worked.

4

You Are Uniquely Qualified

> After all, it's easy to be your first worst critic.
> What's harder—and far more critical—is to
> be your own best champion.
>
> — Melinda Gates

The issue you are facing in the workplace today is not just due to the rapidly changing technology and your lack of ability to keep up. Some of you are doing this well, but still not getting to where you belong. That is because it is not just a skills gap, but a value gap. You have not adequately qualified and quantified your value to your boss and your company.

Your value is unique to you. It is a one-of-a-kind combination of your education, experience, skills, talents, accomplishments, and failures - yes, your failures add to your value, and you will learn more about this later in the book. Your company most likely uses your credentials, as in your college degrees or certifications, to assign a value to you, but they are missing everything else about you. While your value is a unique combination of everything about you, you still have to prove it using a standard. This book, along with its companion website, PaulCarneyWorks.com, will provide you with a standard and tools to qualify and quantify, then promote, your value.

In fact, IBM recently announced that they are shifting from hiring based solely on college degrees to skills-based hiring[13], which means that they are going to also focus on career and technical education (CTE), which is also commonly known as vocational education, when filling skill-based information technology positions. Ginni Rometty, President, and CEO of IBM asserts that IBM is going to create "New Collar" jobs where you don't have to have a university degree to have a job related to technology[14].

"New Collar" jobs are a class of jobs between "Blue Collar" (wage earners whose jobs are performed in work clothes and often involve manual labor)[15] and "White Collar" (workers whose work usually does not involve manual labor and who are often expected to dress with a degree of formality)[16]. The new collar jobs require a specific course of technical or vocational training but not a four-year college degree. Examples of these jobs include dental hygienists and assistants, medical lab technicians, pharmacy technicians, medical assistants, automotive technicians, along with many of the newer information technology fields like cloud computing or network specialists and even data science technicians.

This change also reflects the fact that your credentials, such as a degree or certification, are not directly related to your potential. While some may want to assign a value to you based only on where you have been and what you have done, your value is more than that. It is a combination of credentials and experiences, along with your potential. I will discuss potential later in the book and help you incorporate your potential into your overall career value.

That is not to say that skills are not essential. You need skills to do your job today and to be prepared to handle your job tomorrow. Skills also transfer from position to position, allowing you to adapt to a new role in a new organization quickly. But abilities will only get you so far when it is time for a raise or a promotion. To get the maximum return for your investment of time and energy, you must be able to qualify and quantify your value in terms that the manager and company will understand, agree to and then use to increase your compensation. It is up to you to document it and then tell the story.

Financial teams in a company analyze and maximize profit for the organization. The Human Resources (HR) teams are now creating Human Capital Management (HCM) formulas so that they can do something similar: analyze and maximize the human capital, which is you, your work output and your performance. They are going to create new programs that will attempt to get more efficiency out of you to maximize their considerable investment in you. I will make sure you know your value so that you are not left behind.

Behavior change is up to you. You want easy, fast and personal results. Your results are not only individual but truly one-of-a-kind because they are the unique combination of what you have done to get where you are today. At the same time, while you may not see it this way, much of what you do is noteworthy, even unique or remarkable. When was the last time you did something and found out later that it had more of an impact on someone than you thought it would? You see, you have the ability to impact the environment that surrounds you. Start documenting this impact and you will have two major results.

One, you will better understand how you impact others through your actions and behaviors, which allows you to realize when you are doing it again in the future, and adjust as necessary. If the last time you took action did not get the exact result you wanted, and you find yourself in a similar situation, think before you act this time. Reflect on what you would have done differently because this is a large part of the self-awareness aspect of Emotional Intelligence (EQ), which I will discuss at greater detail later in the book.

The second result you will see from documenting your activity is that you will have an easier time presenting your case when it is time for your performance review. If you are fortunate enough to have reviews with your leader more often than once a year, you will have snippets of information to share each time. If your performance review is once a year, by the time you are ready to provide your input, you will have accumulated a tremendous amount of data from which you can draw the top accomplishments you achieved. It is a lot easier to filter through a lot of data to create a well-crafted list of achievements than it is to stare at a blank page and create the list from scratch. And you, like me, will never remember all of the great things you did if you don't write it down. Our memories cannot store it all.

If you don't currently get a performance review or you are not asked to provide input before your review is given, then you are in the unfortunate group of people, which is larger than you think, who need to take control of your situation and drive the conversation. Remember, it is your career, and it belongs to you, not someone else. It is your responsibility to present your case to receive acknowledgment and any increases in pay or promotions. It will be more work for you than those who have more collaborative bosses, but that makes it that much more vital for you to document your successes and provide your achievements. If that still does not help your boss understand your value, then it may be time to find a new boss. Either way, you are on the road to knowing and showing your career value, which is necessary for you to move ahead in your career and not be left behind.

Potential is tough to measure. To get started, let's look at the definition of potential. By breaking it down, we can set up a process to qualify and quantify the potential component of your value.

Potential is the inherent ability or capacity for growth, development, or future success[17].

Inherent Ability or Capacity

These are latent, or non-visible, qualities and abilities that a person has. There are many reasons why they are not visible, including a lack of opportunity to display them or limited knowledge on how to promote them. And capacity refers to the ability to make or accomplish something, which indicates that the person can expand his capabilities to fill a need.

Growth and Development

These terms refer to the need for continuous learning, a focus on further education through various methods, both formal and informal.

Future Success

Future success is just that: something that can happen, but has not materialized.

That last part of the definition, "future success," is where the most difficulty comes in when trying to measure potential. We have easy ways to review past performance and assign a score. Think of a grade on a school test, a sports team score or the rating you received on your last performance review. They all look at events from the past and produce a measurement based on goals that were set. But what about future events? How do we measure something that has not happened yet? Even more, what is the measuring stick you need to use?

Your vision of where you want to go projects forward. Start from there and look back, which will show you what you need to do to get there. It is better than trying to start from a road you have not traveled yet. See the vision of where you will land, then work backward in your mind to find the way forward. It is much easier than trying to move forward, not seeing where you are going to end up. Your potential is about the future. It is based on activities you have done, but the power of what you can still accomplish lies ahead of you, so why focus solely on the past? Paint the future the way you want it to be and fill in the details during the journey.

Evan Carmichael, the founder of Evan Carmichael Communications Group, has one of the best LinkedIn taglines I have seen. In November 2017, it was this:

I'm working to solve the world's biggest problem: Untapped human potential. Join me. #Believe[18]

Isn't that amazing? He is working to figure out how to pull together all of this unused human potential. This is your call to read further and find a way to develop the formula for your potential so that you can help him solve this worldwide issue.

Simon Sinek said it best at his TED talk at TEDxPuget Sound in September 2009:

...what you do simply serves as the proof of what you believe.[19]

Beyond the "right answers" and success, are you asking the right questions which will drive you down your path? The questions you ask about your value will be an essential factor in your success. Questioning and learning leads to increased value, not just the final score. The most powerful lessons were learned during the game, which is the same with your career. You simply have not been taught how to identify and document your successes. Your teachers and professors wanted you to listen to them, study and pass an exam, but they didn't show you how to document what you learned and build on it in your career. I will show you how to do that.

In that same TEDxPuget Sound talk, Sinek also indicated how important it is for you to know *why* you do what you do:

But if you don't understand why you do what you do, how will you ever get people to be loyal and want to be a part of what it is that you do.[20]

Do you know why you do what you do? I didn't fully understand this either until I heard Sinek phrase it that way. I came up with a list of reasons why I do what I do:

- I interact with people in person and on social media because I am curious and want to learn from them.
- I connect people with each other when I believe each of them can receive value from the relationship.
- I learn, grow and discuss topics with passion because I want to help others grow and develop their abilities.

It was when I put this list together that I realized why I became a high school math teacher at the beginning of my career, why I get such a great feeling leading people who accomplish great things, and why introducing people to each other is so much fun. Be prepared to create a short list of your "why" items at the end of this chapter.

To be successful in promoting your value, you have to know your value and be able to describe it. When I was talking to the many people who helped me during my research for this book, many of them indicated that it sounds like they are bragging if they started listing and talking about their achievements. As I asked a few more questions, I found three major, recurring points:

1. It can sound like I am bragging.
2. It appears that I am being egotistical and that it has to be all about me.
3. By highlighting my accomplishments, it sounds like I am making others feel less worthy.

I will start with the easy one – bullet #2: Yes, it is all about you. There is nothing wrong with doing this, at the right time and in the right way. Remember the story in an earlier chapter where I stated to my daughter that she does not have to follow the rules...as long as she is willing to accept the consequences? Well, it is the same situation for you. You need to focus on you to understand how to get the most value for your career, but it is vital that you do it at the right time and in the right way. Let me give you an example.

You have just been selected for a high-profile project that ultimately includes a presentation to the president of your company. You are so excited and made the time to learn about the project six months ago and did industry research about the topic. You then reached out to your LinkedIn network to ask some questions of people who had completed a similar project. You made sure to mention these efforts to your boss during a one-to-one meeting. You also informed your boss that you are interested in joining the project team, and gave your manager a short, 3-bullet list of why you would add value representing the group on the project.

Your colleague also wanted to be on the project, but he did not do too much to prepare. He did not tell his boss that he wanted to be on the project because the boss knew that he did a similar project eight years ago at another company, and that should be enough to be selected to represent the team. He also has been in the industry for a few decades and feels that his accomplishments are known. Ultimately, you are chosen to represent your team on the project.

Now that you are selected, should you be proud? Yes, you should. Should you tell people how proud you are of what you accomplished? Yes, you should. And that is where the 2-step process comes in: discuss it at the right time and in the right way. For timing, make sure the boss has announced it first. And while it is okay to discuss it for the first 1-3 days after you get selected, that is probably the limit of talking about it in front of your team. There will be plenty of times later when you are applying for another job or with other groups where you can describe how you succeeded in being selected, but after a few days, the story becomes stale and will sound more like bragging.

How you describe your success will have the most significant impact and separate braggadocio from pride. Melinda Gates, the Co-chair of the Bill & Melinda Gates Foundation, discusses how to tackle the "impostor syndrome[21]" where you have a difficult time accepting a success. You doubt that you took the best actions or that your input had a direct impact on the results. In her article, she explains how to recognize these feelings and move past them. When you do this, you begin to understand and celebrate your uniqueness, which is an essential step in your career success.

You can understand why running around the office, arms waving, doing fist pumps, and whooping it up is not the best way to show your pride. Besides, "trash talking" those who were not selected will also give others the perception that you are interested in only yourself and your accomplishments.

When someone congratulates you, say, "thank you" and give them a quick introduction, such as, "I did some extra research, reached out to industry professionals and made sure my boss knew that I wanted to be on the project." By doing it this way, you are not bragging about the accomplishment of being selected, but are instead outlining what you did to **earn** the achievement, which not only helps the other person understand that this was not luck or favoritism, but the result of actions that you took to prepare for success. Your colleague who did not get selected will most likely not talk with you directly about it, but will likely talk with others about his disappointment. If some of those people heard your complete success story and how you got there, they can share with the other colleague to counter any "not fair" perception.

What do you do if that other person does approach you? You give him the same story, but then follow up with, "Do you want to see what I collected and who I talked with?" By doing this, you position yourself as the person who not only achieved a goal, but you are willing to help others achieve, too. Your colleague was resting on his laurels and did not realize that he needed to keep sharp on his skills and discuss thoughts and ideas with other industry professionals to create more value for his career. By helping your colleagues understand what you did, you are providing them with the knowledge of how they can create opportunities for their improvement.

And that is why you are reading this book - to learn how to know, grow and show your value. In fact, when my process works for you, it is your responsibility to help your colleagues learn how they, too, can qualify and quantify their career value so they don't get left behind.

Chapter Debrief

- "New Collar" jobs are between "Blue Collar" and "White Collar" and involve more technical training than college degrees
- Potential looks forward, so project what that can look like and prepare to reach it
- Earn achievements by being prepared and selling yourself

Your Turn

1. Create a list of three reasons **why** you do what you do.

2. List the one professional attribute about you that is the easiest to sell to your leaders.

5

Value Equation Explained

> Strive not to be a success, but rather to be of value.
>
> — Albert Einstein

Before we can calculate your career value, let's look deeper into the concept of value so that you fully understand your value when we put it together. In simple terms, value is defined as:

**worth in goods, services or money
of an object or person**[22]

Seth Godin, the esteemed business author, and speaker, even reminded us of the time-tested formula[23] that helps us understand this concept more clearly:

Value = Benefit / Price

Which reads as "Value equals Benefit divided by Price."

Now, I know that by putting math in my book, I risk you immediately dropping the book to run - but do not do it.

Trust me and stick with me for a few more sentences. You learned earlier that I started my career as a high school math teacher, so rest assured that I will get you through this quick micro-learning session with ease.

Here is an easy way to see how this equation works. Imagine that two people each just bought a new car, with Sam Sedan buying a $18,000 family sedan and the Pat Performance buying a $36,000 performance car. While Pat spent twice as much money, they can both get the same value. Look at the table below, which lists the typical benefits a person gets with each vehicle.

	Benefits
Sam Sedan	- Safe transportation
	- Reliability
	- Good gas mileage
Pat Performance	- Safe transportation
	- Reliability
	- High-end performance
	- Sleek profile
	- Prestigious brand
	- Top-of-the-line sound system

As you can see, Sam was looking for basic car attributes of transportation and reliability. In addition to those, Pat was looking to make a statement and have a ride that had more high-end features which signified prestige and cachet. When we plug this into our formula, we see the following:

Sam:

Value = 3 benefits / \$18,000 = 1 benefit / \$6,000

Pat:

Value = 6 benefits / \$36,000 = 1 benefit / \$6,000

They have the same value of 1 benefit per every \$6,000 they spend. Isn't that interesting? Two people can buy cars for very different prices, yet get the same value.

It happens all over the consumer market, from toys to beds, computers, phones, clothing, and the list goes on. In fact, this value equation also shows why if you are going to ask for more salary from your employer, you better be providing more benefits to them so that they get at least the same value from you. And here is a little secret: They are going to want to get more value from you, which means your benefits must increase faster than the price they are paying you, or your request will be denied. I will help you develop a solid value statement.

One interesting sidebar to this equation is this: What happens when Price = 0? Do you remember your math teacher explaining that you cannot divide by zero? She was right. We say that when you try to divide a real number by zero, you get an undefined answer, meaning that there is no answer. So, if the price is zero in our value equation above, we get an undefined value.

That does not mean that everything that is free has no specific value, but it does help show that by paying a price, you get value. In your case, you have to invest some time and most likely a little money to increase your career value. I will help you develop a plan as to the best way for you to balance these needs and answer that question. This formula is essential for you to understand as you continue reading, as it is the foundation of how you are going to increase your career value.

Your value is built incrementally and compounds over time, like interest in your investment account. Have you heard of compounding interest and how it turns $100 today into tens of thousands decades later? That is due to compounding interest, where you earn interest on your original money and its interest. Your career value has the same compounding effect. But you have to start today with the small investment. Once you do, compounding has already begun.

If you, as the worker, are not adding value and feel valued in your role, your productivity will decline. Don't let that happen to you. Learn what value you add today, what value you can add tomorrow, then do it.

Chapter Debrief

- Understanding the value equation helps you prepare your Æ

- Before you ask for a raise, you need to develop the additional benefits you will provide to generate equal or greater value for their investment in you

- Like investments, your value can take advantage of compounding over time

Your Turn

1. Create a list of five benefits you provide to your company in your current role.

2. Using the list from above, create the value that you provide in a year for those benefits:
    Value = 5 / (your annual salary)

MOVE YOUR Æ

6

Know Your Resources

> Successful careers are not planned. They
> develop when people are prepared for
> opportunities because they know their
> strengths, their method of work, and their
> values.
>
> — Peter Drucker

It is up to you to assume control and be accountable for your future. Do not hand that responsibility to others. I remember the day that my 11-year-old daughter, Elizabeth, brought home a grade that she had earned in a middle school class. It was a grade that did not meet the standards that my wife and I had set. When my wife began to have a conversation with her about the grade, my daughter moved quickly into the classic, rebellious 11-year-old stance and stated, "Why do you care what grade I get?" Ah, there it was, the moment for me to impart some wisdom that she did not see coming.

I asked my daughter to sit on the couch, then sat next to her and calmly started the conversation. "Elizabeth, let me explain to you why your grades are important to you. Your mother and I have already earned our high school diplomas and achieved the grades we needed to graduate from college, even get a Master's Degree. We have our solid foundation for our future careers. Your grades are an important part of your future career. Mom and I want you to be very successful, which is why we set these higher standards." I paused for a minute for her to let the concept settle in, then continued, "You see, we want the best for you and will support you, but it is up to you to earn the good grades, then get into good schools so that you can earn a degree. In a nutshell, your grades and your future are yours, not ours."

So, I impart the same wisdom to you, my reader. Your value and your future are yours. Do not hand it over to someone else, whether that is your boss or your company. You have to take responsibility to improve and keep up yet to do this; there is one small change you may have to make in your weekly routine. I know - here I am in the first few chapters of the book and I am already asking you to change. Leadership training tells me that it may be too early for me to ask you to take action, but I feel it is vital for you to know this one gem before you continue reading. It will be a tool that you use throughout the rest of this book and in your daily life.

Here it is: When faced with a task or a request to complete something, you instantly start to come up with the obstacles that are going to stand in the way. As soon as you have a few (which can be a mere 1-4 seconds), your face starts to form a frown, perhaps even a scowl, and you reassuringly state, "We will not be able to do that."

When we are asked to muster our resources to accomplish something, whether it is a single task by one person or an entire project with a team, our human inclination is to jump to the reasons why it cannot be done. It's related to the limbic brain, which is where the "fight or flight" processing occurs. In this case, you are making sure you have what it takes to fight, or you will have to prepare to run away from the situation. Don't blame yourself too much, as it is a natural instinct honed by your ancestors for thousands of years. You simply have not been made aware that you are having this immediate reaction. But now that you are aware let's work on the way you can change this reaction for sustained success.

Instead of thinking about what cannot be done, ask yourself, "What can we accomplish with the resources we have?" See the difference in the way you are now approaching the situation? Before you would focus on the obstacles, the resources you did not have, and then come to the conclusion that it could not be done. As someone who learned long again to think the opposite, I can tell you that it works very well when you take a creative look at the resources you do have and try to figure out what can be done.

Why is this the case? Because it turns into a puzzle or a mystery, which is something to be solved. That now sounds a little fun, doesn't it? Also, it is now a challenge. If you can figure out how far you can get with the resources available, you will be seen as a resourceful person and perhaps even rewarded, even if you did not make it all of the way to the finish line.

To get started on this mindset, you have to assess the situation and assemble three things quickly:

- What am I being asked to accomplish and why?
- What resources do I have available?
- What flexibility do I have?

Once you have those, you now start solving the puzzle of how you are GOING to GET IT DONE.

Start with the goal. Who wants this task done and why? What is their vision for the final product? These things are important to know so that if you do not have everything you need to get started, you are aware of what you have to ask for to reach the final target.

As you assess your current resources, start to put together the phrase, "We could do X if we had Y." That framework allows you to flip from not being able to accomplish the task to informing your boss or project manager what you will be able to do, with the specific resources, time and plan you have worked out. You are in a much better position to negotiate for more time, resources or flexibility to break the project up into phases or modify the ultimate vision. By using this framework, you will learn how to balance realities with possibilities in ways that others will not see at first.

The best way to approach the use of resources is to use an incremental or agile process. You will not identify everything you need at first, but it is important to pick a resource and start. Successful people will tell you to try often, no matter if you fail or succeed. You are going to fail many times. It is up to you to review what happened, and then move on.

Repeat this try and fail-or-succeed process often. You will not only learn from each result, but your success will generate recognition from others, which can open doors to more resources. When evaluating what action you can take in a specific work situation, be sure to use actions that add (+) instead of ones that will take away (-) value. It is easy to fall into the trap of highlighting what is wrong and needs fixing. Flip the sign in your equation to a positive "+" one for better results. Using your resources wisely will signal to others that you are adding value.

I recall one time that my wife, daughter and I were playing a board game called "Stop Thief!". It was one of the first board games to have an electronic component that interacted with you during the game and one that both my wife and I had when we were younger.

In the game, you are a detective using clues to track down a thief before your opponents, and some cards provide you with resources, like extra tips or the ability to move to different locations. The key to catching the thief is that you have to be on a square touching where you thought the thief was located to attempt to place the thief "under arrest" on the electronic device.

My 9-year-old daughter was quite good at the game and was keenly aware of how valuable the resources were. In one particular case, she rolled the two die and got a total of 9 dots, which meant she could move nine spots in any direction. She was also ready to play a resource card, and in this case, she had the golden one: Move Anywhere. She proudly flipped over the card as part of her turn, picked up her detective playing piece, placed him on a spot that was a few squares away from where she wanted to be, then moved her nine spots for the roll of the die. My wife and I looked at each other, wondering why she was doing that since she had the "Move Anywhere" card.

When we asked her why she did that, she replied, "I wanted to make sure I moved the nine spots I got on my roll." She was clear that she was not going to leave any of her resources that she had available on the table. From that point on, the family refers to the "Move Anywhere...Plus 9" concept when we are using resources to get things done.

Being flexible in your approach to situations and challenges takes practice, but once you can negotiate (you will see more on this later), you will be amazed at the flexibility you can create, perhaps breaking up the task or project into phases if there are constraints on timelines or when a person may be available to assist.

The ability to negotiate is so essential to understanding and promoting your career value. It is how you can improve your performance, increase your value and earn more money. Along with this comes marketing and selling. You have to be able to "toot your own horn" because no one else is going to do it for you that much. You have a story to tell and a case to make for why your value is so important. The ability to persuade someone that you have value in a specific situation is what separates very successful people from all others.

Does this mean that you need to follow the well-worn cliché "think outside the box" to do this? Absolutely not. In fact, I want to help you qualify and quantify what is IN THE BOX that is called YOU. It contains a lot of history, and I want to expose it to the world as your career value. Are you ready?

**If you cannot quantify your value,
how do you expect others to do it?**

Chapter Debrief

- Your career is yours – do not hand control to others

- Flip the focus of your questions to concentrate on what you can accomplish with the resources you have

- Negotiate for additional resources as needed, but be sure to follow the "Move Anywhere...Plus 9" mantra to consume all supplies available

Your Turn

1. Think of the last time you did not have enough people, time or money to accomplish a goal. Flip the focus and create a list of two ways you could have accomplished something using the resources you did have.

2. Create a list of three things that you lack in your job to be the most effective you can be.

MOVE YOUR Æ

7

What is the Æ?

A mind that is stretched by new experiences can never go back to its old dimensions.

—Oliver Wendell Holmes, Jr.

According to Wikipedia[24], the Æ (pronounced "ash") was originally a ligature representing the Latin diphthong "ae" and is now a letter in the alphabet of some languages. If any of you are like me, that is about all I want to know about the Æ, except that it is going to be the symbol for your career value. If you want to learn more about its roots or symbolism, check out the link in the footnote.

Why did I pick the Æ? It appeared to me when I was doing my original research for speeches I was preparing to give at two technology conferences in the fall of 2017. The speeches were titled, "Human vs. Robot: How You Will Win." I needed a character that could easily be written or typed which would represent the value you will need to acquire to win against the automation of your job (the robot). Most of the characteristics I came up with like acumen, ability, aptitude, attitude, engagement, empowerment and emotional intelligence, started with an "a" or an "e," so when I saw the Æ, I was intrigued. When I saw that it was called an "ash," I was hooked. Like an emoji, it is a simple expression for a complex idea.

It was while preparing for the speeches that I began to bring together the concept that was missing for so many of us:

We have not been able to qualify and quantify our career value effectively.

Many business people, educators, and leaders were staring at the charts wondering how wages can remain stable with little to no growth, while unemployment continued to drop and job openings continue to jump. It is an economist's bad dream in trying to explain this because standard economic theory states that when supply decreases (fewer workers available to fill the growing list of job openings), demand increases, which will cause prices (wages) to rise to fill the demand.

To groups focused on the "skills gap" that was apparent. As efficiencies created by automation was replacing workers, they did not have the skills needed in today's high-demand jobs, such as technicians, analysts and many fields within information technology, especially around artificial intelligence (AI) and cybersecurity. Many programs have been created to retrain or "upskill" these workers so that they could take on these new roles.

But it still did not sit well with me. Having managed the worldwide talent acquisition team for a large, financial company (which has been on Fortune's 100 Best Companies to Work For[25] List for numerous years) and reviewing my almost 30 years as an adult in the working world, I kept feeling that it was more than just skills. People I knew who had excellent skills and abilities were being passed up for opportunities that seemed to be a good fit. I started to see contradictory reasons given by hiring leaders for not choosing very-qualified candidates. The process was designed to remove bias, so I was beginning to realize that we were missing something and I was going to find out what it was.

The first step to determining your career value was to qualify what constitutes "value" in a career. Remember from a previous chapter that value is defined as "worth in goods, services or money of an object or person[26]." In your case, your career value is a unique representation of your worth in the job marketplace. It combines your skills, education, talents, experiences, failures, trials, achievements and rewards. Just like two equally-sized snowflakes that are unique in their ice pattern, no two human career values are alike, but they can have the same measured value.

For example, two friends go to different high schools and play basketball. When they graduate from high school, each is offered a full scholarship to play basketball at similar colleges in the same athletic division. In terms of the value of their high school career and ability to earn a full scholarship for college using their basketball talents, they achieve a similar value, but their journey to get there looks very different. Your Æ (ash) is your own but can have the same quantity as another person's Æ.

The next step is to quantify those qualities, and that is where the Æ comes into play. If you are going to build and increase value, you have to have a foundation on which to start and measures in place to determine if the value is changing, and in which direction it is changing. Like a good compass, you need to understand where True North lies, then use the changes in the direction indicated by the compass to be sure you are on the right path in your journey.

The Æ is your measurement by which you will document and promote your career's journey.

While your Æ is a comprehensive collection of everything about you that has driven you in your career, there are a few characteristics that I cover in this book to get you started. In fact, in honor of the Æ being the combination of the letters "A" and "E," I have chosen three qualities for each of those letters to begin your journey.

Here are three "A" attributes:

Acumen

Acumen is the ability to make good judgments on any given topic. A professional in a given domain is called a "Subject Matter Expert" or SME. For you, this is the strength you have in knowledge and experience for a given subject. The judgments you make are based on what you have done before and the results you witnessed.

One of the downsides of too much business acumen is that you may get trapped in thinking only within the silo of your expertise for solutions to problems when there are innovative ways that can be borrowed from other areas to solve issues in your area. That insulated thought process is why it is essential to network and collaborate with professionals in other fields.

Awareness

The level of your awareness represents how well you can view and perceive the events that are occurring around you. On the one hand, you can track and manage the facts of a situation, such as there was ice on the road or the band was playing music. On the other side, you develop stories about the facts, such as that is why the car slid off the road or that you got this great feeling because the song that the band was playing was one that you remember from your childhood. The depth of awareness is affected by how engaged you are with the activities going on around you.

The most important aspect of awareness for you and your career is self-awareness, which is your ability to know how you impact the environment around you through your actions and words. People who have strong self-awareness can more easily persuade and influence actions around them because they understand how to present themselves and their ideas in ways that others will agree. Strong self-awareness means that no matter how you think your idea should be expressed, how the other parties are receiving the message is what matters most. It requires you to have a high-performing feedback system to accomplish this.

Ability

Your ability is centered on your talents and skills. Your talents are built-in, natural tendencies that you have. These are the things that you do without even thinking because it naturally feels right to you. Coaches who identify talent and help a person develop their abilities have the highest impact on talent. Great coaches know how to challenge a talented person to improve their ability to be able to compete at the highest levels. You have seen this happen in sports, music, and acting.

The cousin to talent is skill. We have all developed skills in our lives, from learning to write the letters of the alphabet and add numbers to learning how to drive a vehicle or use our thumbs to text on a smartphone. In this case, we rely on teachers to show us how to begin using the skill, and we get better through additional practice and instruction from the teacher.

Given the wide range of skills that are available for you to learn in life, your aptitude or proclivity to understand and learn will lead you to advance more quickly. A great welder not only has to understand how electricity creates heat to forge a bond through molten metals, but she also needs the dexterity to hold the welding gun steady and keep it moving along the path to create a solid, rolling bead that delivers a strong bond and looks good. Having welded many times in my life, I say that I have the skill to weld, but the jagged bead along the edges of my work proves that I have quite a bit of practice to achieve before I can be considered a highly-skilled welder.

And here are three "E" attributes to focus on:

Engagement

It is difficult to grow and learn without being engaged. Don't just sit on the sidelines. Jump in and join the conversation, but that does not mean you have to become an outgoing extrovert who is always connecting with people. It means that you have to show some passion and excitement for the activity you are about to start. Get rid of the other distractions and focus on what you are learning. For classroom-based instructions, this means putting your smartphone on silent and ignoring it. I know that it can be difficult to do, but you will short-change your ability to develop your career value if you allow others to manage your time for you, especially when you are focused on learning.

Empowerment

Empowerment embodies having the authority to take control over your life. I don't have the power to do this, because it belongs to you. As you develop the confidence to make changes in your life, it gets easier for you to build your skills and career. I know that it is not easy for you to get out of your "comfort zone" because it is safe in there and you know what you are doing. But the challenge is that while you stay in that confined zone, the world is rapidly changing around you. Innovation and new skills are happening out there, and for you to tap into those opportunities, you have to venture out of your comfort zone.

My suggestion is that you do this one small step at a time. You do not have to jump both feet from 100 feet above the cliff. Instead, identify one new skill you want to develop and work on it a few hours a week. That is all - just a few hours at a time. Before you know it, you will have the strength to take on more and your comfort zone will soon expand.

I have lived this for myself as I wrote this book. While I like to write, taking on an entire book is a daunting task. I found a few tools like Scrivener and set a goal of writing 1,000 words a day. To most that would seem like a lot, but for me, I knew it was within my abilities. Yes, there were some evenings when I would be at home, exhausted from the efforts I expended during the day working with people to help advance their careers, but I found the strength to get it done, and I know that you can, too.

EQ or EI (Emotional Intelligence)

Emotional Intelligence is the ability for you to identify your emotions and the emotions of those around you so that you can modify your reactions and behaviors to affect the situation[27]. It is commonly represented as "EI." It is also quantified as "EQ," which stands for "Emotional Quotient," and is designed to be a companion to "IQ" or "Intelligence Quotient." No matter which abbreviation you use, it is an important concept to understand as it will allow you to know how you can manage your emotions and reactions in all aspects of your life, including at work.

Before I became a certified practitioner of the MBTI® Step I and Step II instruments and the EQ-i 2.0® instrument in 2013, I had a solid understanding of my emotional responses, especially in business. But the training taught me many more ways to develop stronger strategies to both identify and manage my emotions. While it is outside the scope of this book to cover all of the aspects of these strategies, I will cover the basic concepts to get you started.

Your personality is the combination of traits that are meant to predict how you will behave in different situations. Since you continue to develop as you mature, it helps to understand how your personality as an adult is related to your temperament as an infant and toddler[28]. One typical assumption among the scientific community is that the traits that define your personality cannot be readily modified, but recent research is beginning to show how you can choose to modify your personality traits[29].

Personality assessments are testing instruments that are used to identify how your personality traits affect your interactions within your environment. These assessments were initially developed to assist with personnel selection. Most instruments today may be used to identify characteristics of careers in which you may excel. Yet these traits are not typically legitimized for the employees selected for a specific job. If you are asked to take a personality assessment as part of a job application process, ask for details on validating the evaluations for this selection, and the hiring team should point you to an online source that contains the validation data.

There are a wide variety of assessments available. Here is a short list of the most common you may encounter:

- Thematic Apperception Test
- Minnesota Multiphasic Personality Inventory (MMPI)
- Five Factor Model (FFM) or Big Five personality traits
- Myers-Briggs Type Indicator (MBTI)
- The 16PF Questionnaire (16PF)
- The Personality and Preference Inventory (PAPI)
- The Newcastle Personality Assessor (NPA)
- DiSC® assessment
- The NEO PI-R, or the Revised NEO Personality Inventory

I have seen the MBTI and DiSC assessments be instrumental in business. I worked at a large organization that had an award-winning learning and development group who used both of these assessments to help individuals learn more about themselves and why they interact and react the way that they do in work situations. I was amazed as we watched the revelation on people's faces when they could connect a specific way that they act to their personality traits. Even more powerful was when we would discuss how their personality traits affected their contributions to a team. Many participants could recall a time when they either worked well with or struggled to communicate with a colleague. We would walk them through the concept that neither person is right or wrong, but that this deeper level of introspection allows them to understand each other better and they can adjust how they work with one another for more effective results.

One of the most widely available models for emotional intelligence is the EQ-i 2.0 instrument[30]. The EQ-i 2.0 Model includes one overarching score comprised of five composite scores, which are then broken down into a total of 15 subscales.

The five composite scores reflect areas such as:

- Self-Perception
- Self-Expression
- Interpersonal
- Decision Making
- Stress Management

Among those five areas are measurements for attributes such as:

- Self-Regard
- Assertiveness
- Empathy
- Problem Solving
- Stress Tolerance

I can spend a whole book describing how vital understanding your personality traits and emotional intelligence are to your career. My goal is to introduce you to the concepts so that you can do further research. In fact, why not make taking one of these assessments as a way for you to grow your career? Keep that in mind when you get to the end of this chapter.

I mentioned previously that the concept of the Æ evolved during the research for speeches I gave at technology conferences. In those speeches, I covered another statement that is important for you to understand:

We need to embrace our egos, fears, and humility to move our Æ

For my speeches at the technology conferences, I was speaking to a highly-technical and specialized audience. These are people whose skills are in high demand in a rapidly changing industry. As I asked them if they were ready to battle the robots for their jobs, I presented that statement to remind them that while they may be the top of their field today, they have to continuously improve to stay ahead.

The same sentiment applies to you, because you have to be keenly aware how the innovative technological changes in the workplace will not only change the way that you work, but it may replace what you do. It is not a complete horror story for you, the human, though. As Peter Drucker, the well-known management consultant, educator, and writer stated,

Effectiveness should be a human pursuit, while efficiency should be delegated to machines.[31]

For you, this means that you need to make sure your value is more on the effectiveness scale than the efficiency scale. To support this statement, I gave the audiences my top three ways that I believe you, as a human, can provide effective value and keep an edge over computers for at least the next five years. Starting from the bottom of the list:

#3 Curiosity

Inquisitiveness is a natural animal instinct which robots have not developed yet. We can program computers to run simulations and learn from them, or even attempt to work out every possibility to solve a problem like winning the game of chess or Go, but genuine curiosity comes from the desire to learn. I have not seen a computer express desire yet.

Curiosity is how we learn and build experiences. It is the unique way that you look at the world. While I see a shade of blue, you may see purple, and that can affect our curiosity, especially if one of those is our favorite color. Curiosity leads to inspiration and discovery, from solving problems to wanting to learn more about something or someone. The love between human beings is one great example where curiosity leads to the desire to want to discover more about another person and be together for a longer time. Apples have always fallen from trees, and Sir Isaac Newton wasn't the first to wonder why, but he was the person who developed and tested statements to figure out why the apples fell. It is that curiosity that led to his conclusions and formulas about gravity, which we still use today.

#2 Empathy

Technically, empathy is the capacity for you to understand how another person is feeling, specifically from their perspective. Think of it as being able to put yourself in their situation, given their background and experiences, and knowing how they will react. On a more personal level, empathy is about using that understanding to develop relationships and networks of support through a stronger recognition and tolerance of how each of our unique values brings different aspects to the relationship and situation.

People with strong empathy will have an easier time learning effective ways to motivate people because they can comprehend the subtleties of how the other person operates, or as we colloquially say, "what makes them tick." Your ability to persuade someone to recognize your value will rely heavily on having empathy, too.

#1 Creativity

Finally, the top attribute that you have and a computer does not is creativity, which is your ability to imagine, design and innovate. While computers can come up with novel ideas to problems or even use networks constructed to represent neural networks, they are not (yet) capable of creating innovative ideas from struggles and adversity. One way that I have been creative in my career is that I created a non-linear future by varying the types of jobs and industries in which I have worked.

While this may have limited my ability to climb the proverbial corporate ladder at one company, I was able to bring ideas from one job to another, thereby adding an atypical value. Until now, it was difficult to quantify this value. Don't be afraid to bob-and-weave and zig-and-zag in your career. Go ahead and take the road not taken. At the same time, remember to

Dream Big, Get Stuff Done and Have Fun!

The more you know yourself, the more others can know about you. And by learning techniques to understand others, including how and why they operate the way that they do, you will be able to create relationships in which you can work more effectively together. This deeper and broader understanding of how to be effective in teams adds a tremendous amount of value to your Æ.

Want to learn how to type the Æ on your mobile device or computer? Check out page 212 for the easy instructions.

Now that you know the concepts behind the Æ let's look at how to manage it for your career.

Chapter Debrief

- The Æ is used to qualify and quantify your career value

- Humans have more impact when we focus on effectiveness and learn to work with machines that can operate more efficiently

- Curiosity, Empathy and Creativity are characteristics of humans that robots have not emulated – yet

Your Turn

1. List three ways that you and a machine work well together.

2. Review the list of available personality and leadership assessments and pick one that you will allocate the time and money to take. Then, write down a date by which you will complete the assessment.

8

Your Career Æ

The biggest mistake that you can make is to believe that you are working for somebody else.

— Earl Nightingale

Just as you have had various experiences, jobs, and groups of friends in your life, your career has multiple types of value. Your value can be expressed for your experiences, education, skills, talents and other attributes across many different dimensions, including your:

- Company
- Team
- Profession
- Industry
- Geography

It is this particular matrix of values that make your career unique. Do not let others tell you that they have a sure fire way to define your value unless they can help you express your uniqueness across those many dimensions. You need a tool that will help you quantify and qualify your unique value across those dimensions in comparison to others. You need a guide or a coach, not a one-size-fits-all solution. You need to incorporate your passion and energy into your Æ.

You are likely thinking that this can get very complex. I would be lying to you if I said that is not true, as we are complicated beings that are a result of everything we have experienced, our beliefs and our morals. But please allow me to reassure you that I can help you know, grow and show your career value, your Æ, in simple ways. Let's take an example of one aspect of society where there is a lot of data collected and analyzed from which standard means of measurements are created to compare one unit to another. That example is the world of sports.

From little league to the ranks of athletic professionals, we collect a lot of data about the games we play, especially at the professional levels. We now collect not only how many yards a U.S. football player rushes or how many sacks a defensive player makes on the quarterback, but we track the conditions of the day of play, including the temperature, dew point, status of the sunshine and even the condition of the turf. Here are just a few of the items for one professional U.S. football game:

- Weather
- Team roster (including who was injured or ill)
- Coaching roster
- Player statistics
- Referee group
- Home/Away game

And the list goes on.

If you watch any professional sport now on television, including football, they will have statistics for many combinations of previous events. Including the record of every time the two teams have met before, the quarterback's entire set of statistics on passing completions, interceptions and various other accomplishments against this team, even possibly against the current players on the defensive line.

While some of this information is for entertainment or "Did You Know?" value, some of it is not as relevant as you may believe. For instance, just because one team has beaten the other team ten times and lost two times in the previous 12 meetings, those teams most likely consisted of different players, possibly even different coaches, so the correlation between the previous wins and their chance of winning this time may not be that solid.

A lot of the data is relevant to understanding the value of a player, a team and the games that they play. Billy Beane, the larger-than-life Oakland Athletics baseball team general manager, faced a very lean budget with which he and his coaching staff had to assemble players to compete with the powerhouse clubs like the New York Yankees. As the story goes, he came to an epiphany one day and realized that the methods that teams were using were outdated and had not caught up with modern advances in analytical technology.

As a result, he threw out the traditional and widely-accepted player statistics like bases stolen and batting averages. Instead, he and his coaching staff conducted rigorous statistical methods across many player performance data and found that other factors, like slugging percentage and on-base percentage, especially when combined, provided a more significant ability to predict player, and in turn, team, success. This story is in the popular book and movie titled, Moneyball[32].

In the end, the final score of the game or championships won is the record we remember. But those numbers are but just one measure of success. For sporting events, we know that it is also important to know who contributed what value during the game. So many people add value, on the field, the sidelines, and during preparations for the game. These behind-the-scenes crews and support teams have a large impact on the players and teams' ability to win. And teams will watch recordings of the games afterward to learn how each player contributed to the game, how the other teams played, and what they can do differently next time. Each coach and player watches their performance to analyze and learn what they can do to improve the next time.

Just as the game's play is documented and statistics are captured for each event, recording your career Æ is your way of keeping score of your career. Your latest performance score, merit raise or promotion is just one piece of the story. There are many other things that you do each day and week, but unlike professional sports, there are not teams of people watching and recording your achievements and failures. You might say that your boss is doing that, and she might be doing it in a small way, but the real value of what you add is hidden from view. Just as Billy Beane came up with a way to quantify the actual data that made a difference in player performance, documenting your career value is how you can uncover the hidden attributes that lead to your success. Once you have this data, you can now more easily promote your value and be selected for the next, winning team.

Similar to how professional sports teams have scouts who are continually watching and looking for their next talent from different labor pools, good company recruiters are also doing this. You have to build this set of data about you and your career value, then promote it so that the recruiters can find you. Do you have a worksheet of your stats like a basketball, football or baseball player does? Why not? Most likely because you have not had an easy way to do this, until now.

Your career Æ is about more than just your professional development at one company because your career Æ is portable. You own it, not your company, and you can take it no matter where your career takes you. It helps you remain agile, nimble and able to quickly display your value to other groups when you are looking to join a new team. In fact, if you are one of the more than 36% who consider themselves "Freelance Workers,"[33] then your career Æ is what you need while building your value in the marketplace.

The "Gig Economy," where freelance workers take more control over their future work situations, is growing around the world, especially in the United States[34]. As the article in the footnote indicates, the main takeaway for why people are choosing this lifestyle is freedom and flexibility. With that freedom comes the responsibility of the individual to now define, track and promote her value. She can no longer depend on climbing the usual corporate ladder, where the company determines your value by placing you on a professional or leadership track, dictating how and what you do. She can now take control of her work and how she defines her value, which is what documenting your Æ is designed to do.

The workers in the "gig economy" include not only freelancers but professional small business people and the self-employed. Let's assume that this entire group of workers falls into three categories:

1. Those people who actively select this work situation for the flexibility and autonomy

2. Those who cannot find a regular, full-time job that suits their needs

3. Those who work at least one job already and take on this extra work for supplemental income

In all three cases, the worker must be able to qualify his value in the marketplace to maximize the compensation he receives. Often, business owners and freelancers will worry about the rates they should charge. Too often, they have it backward. They need to focus on the value they provide, then charge a price for which the consumer gets the best value.

If value = benefit/price, then price = benefit/value (a little math for you). If you bring a lot of value but little benefit to the user, it will be difficult to charge a high price. But, if your value is high and the benefit of that value is higher, you can charge top rates.

Another aspect of the gig economy is that more individuals and groups are banding together to create mutuals and cooperatives to provide a higher level of total value through the summation of each person's contributions. In these new types of work cooperatives, there is no bureaucracy of a command-and-control management system through which all decisions funnel. The value of the group is determined by an algorithm that includes the relationships and the work accomplishments. For you to take advantage of this new work capability, you have to be able to define your value in quantifiable terms.

Have you ever heard the phrase, "The sum of the whole is much more than the sum of the individuals?" Did you ever stop to think about what they mean? If you have five people, and they contribute one unit of value to a team but work alone at their tasks, then you add them up and get five total units of work produced by the team. But, what if the group works together, sharing ideas and building on each other's points. You have seen this happen before. It is when the group finishes a set of tasks and says, "I wouldn't have thought to do that." You get great value from a group of individuals that work together when they share and build on concepts. The same is true for your career. In this book, you are not only focusing on your value but the value that you bring to teams, interconnecting the entire career journey.

Were you taught to color in the lines when you were a child? How about the command to sit quietly in your chair during class or not talk with anyone or consult with others when doing your homework or a test? Is that how you accomplish tasks at work today? No. In fact, the speed of change in today's working world requires that we work together on solutions or others will overtake us. Just as we know that most politics are local, so is your Æ. It is not something that is pushed down to you from someone in a higher position of authority in your organization. It is your Æ, and you are building it from the ground up, aggregating each piece of the puzzle as you go. You will then broadcast it for all to see.

The leaders of your company, under the direction of the Human Resources (HR) leaders, are looking for performance, efficiency, and alignment of you with their goals. They take a top-down approach where their goals are determined, and then they attempt to find where you fit in. In many cases, they do not have the data they need to understand your full career value, so you are overlooked or worse, terminated because they were not able to calculate your value. By developing your Æ, you can show where you fit in.

Do other employees see you as a competitor for their job? They should. When you take this view, you are required to keep moving your Æ while they sit on theirs. You may not want their job, but by thinking and building a strategy around this concept, you remain aware and open to the possibilities more than they do.

Stand up, stand out,
and be counted for your actual value.

Successful people keep company with other successful people. Build your Æ and become part of the network of people who are doing the same. You will support each other as you learn and grow. You will become part of the Top 10%, and you will have new opportunities available to you. Like compounding interest in your bank account, your career Æ will grow in a compounding way, placing you well ahead of your competition.

To accomplish this, you have to be able to compare your value to others in the marketplace. Do not confuse your career value with self-identity or self-worth, as those are very different things. You may not have the best athletic prowess or be one of the most intelligent people in the room, but you still add your value, especially in your career. You must find, document and calculate   that value for others to understand and accept.

Your career Æ will ebb and flow. Your rate of growth and change in Æ will vary according to your place in life and resources you have to spend on your career efforts. Life is more than just a career. For a reminder, refer to my list of priorities at the beginning of Chapter 3. But no matter how much effort you are expending on your career, you must not ignore it, as you will then allow others to manage it. You are in control of your career. You don't need to micro-manage it. You need to find the "just right" allocation that works for you now. As long as you are on track in your plan, your career value will continue to grow.

The perception others have of you matters, and it is based solely on their assumptions and beliefs. It is the judgment that others make of you based on what they know, so you need a way to show them more about you and your value to set the world straight that you are more than just a bag of skills because you have Æ value.

**The more you know yourself,
the more others can know about you.**

Chapter Debrief

- Your career Æ has multiple dimensions
- Recording your career Æ is your way of keeping score of your career, similar to professional sports
- The gig economy, freelancing and work cooperatives require you to have a deeper understanding of the value you add to a team

Your Turn

1. If a talent scout (recruiter) called you, what three things would you want her to know about your career Æ?

2. On a scale from 1-10, with 1 being "not likely" and 10 being "highly likely," what is the value you would give for this question:

> How likely are you to join the Gig Economy in the next five years?

9

Why You Need to Know Your Æ

> Success today requires the agility and drive to constantly rethink, reinvigorate, react, and reinvent.
>
> — Bill Gates

Whose responsibility is it to understand your value - you or the people with whom you are dealing? If you don't take the time to document your value, how do you expect others to recognize it and reward you for it? If you rely on others to understand your significance based on their observations, then you have handed them control of the future of your career, which may be why you are in your current situation.

Think about a job interview. Is it up to the recruiters and hiring managers to understand your value? If you answered yes, then what if they are close-minded about a specific value of your career or are incompetent and do not understand the true value you provided in a previous role? Do you still want to leave that responsibility of understanding to them?

No, you do not. You must assume the accountability to make your value clear and understandable for the current audience. Think of a teacher. Is it her responsibility to help the students learn or is it up to the students to understand the information based on the way that the teacher chooses to introduce the material? It is up to the teacher to present the information in a way that allows for the students to learn, and that means using different tools depending on the group's learning capabilities.

As another example of support for why you want to control the story of your career value, think back to your childhood days when you played "telephone." Children sat in a circle, then started the game by whispering a phrase to the person on the left, then having that person repeat it to the person to his left until the message gets to the final person. Even with a small group, the last message typically ends up being different from the first. And given the complexity of the topic and words used, it can end up a very different message.

Interpretation of a message causes this phenomenon. Along the way, each person physically hears the message through her ears, interprets it in her brain, then expresses the message to the next person from her mouth, using the context and framework in which she understood the information she heard. Her expression of the message is influenced by her past experiences, exposure to ideas and thoughts and even personality. As that happens along every stop on the circle, you can imagine how quickly the original message can be changed and distorted.

Make sure when describing your value to an audience, you manage the message, to interpret it as close to your true intentions as possible. Understanding your audience's history and experiences helps you to accomplish this. It is your responsibility to research the background of any hiring managers who will be interviewing you so that you know enough about them to understand how each of them will interpret your education and experiences, and prepare your message so that it supports your intention. Just as it is your interview and you control the conversation, your career value is yours, and it is up to you to develop and show your Æ.

Knowing and tracking your Æ is an ongoing process that provides dividends every day. Record your accomplishments continuously to make it more timely, relevant and powerful to your career advancement. You must manage your career strategically, taking the small, incremental steps that help you keep up with the changes and keep your job. And the context of your Æ depends on the context of your work situation, including the people, teams, projects, and workload. Not only will this book help you qualify and quantify your career value, you can then help others quantify and qualify their career value, which in turn raises yours.

And even though you get training and gain experience at one company, there is no easy way to translate it to a value that is recognized elsewhere. Your Æ is transferable to anywhere in the world. It allows you the freedom and flexibility to maximize your value to a group or organization, which will, in turn, allow them to pay you more. By knowing your Æ, you show that you have agility and can translate the value you bring from one situation to the next.

You also show that you can continue learning and growing and that you can keep up with the changing workplace demands. The methods described in this book are the easy way for you to document your unique value in a standard format that others will understand. The easier you make it for others to understand your value, the more quickly you can be compensated for it.

Successful people understand to separate the situations in life that they can control from the ones that they cannot. While it is not always a simple "yes" or "no" answer, quickly determining your level of control over a situation allows you to understand the actions you need to take and keep you from reacting in ways that can hamper your future success.

Here is a list of work situations that are most likely outside your control:

- Merger/acquisition of your company
- Termination of your job (beyond reasons for integrity or poor performance)
- Change in your leadership chain

For each of those situations, there is little to nothing you can do to control the change. And while you can plan for them, many of those happen without much notice to you. In this case, you need to be aware that these changes may happen to you and prepare a plan to directly govern the aspects of your career that you can manage to move forward from a sudden, jarring change in your job.

Here is a list of work situations that you can control:

- How you react to a change
- How you manage your career value
- Your attitude

Whether you were aware of an upcoming change or a situation you thought was going to go north instead went south, it is how you react to the situation that will make the difference in how it supports or detracts from your success. Typically, highly-emotional-intelligent people know that you should not react immediately to a change. Barring a life-or-death situation, no one should be running down the hall, hands in the air as if their hair is on fire. Learning how to react calmly to change is an essential step to success.

As you learn from the topics in this book, it is critical that you understand how important your attitude is to your career value. Everything you do or say sprouts from the attitude you have at that time. Think about a time you were upset with someone, and you did not want to talk with him, but you had to share information that he needed to complete his work. How you share this information with him will come directly from your attitude, and in most cases, will not be a pleasant interaction. Everyone around you, from your peers to your boss, will evaluate your career value based on your actions.

Instead, imagine if you realized how important your attitude is, took a deep breath, and recognized that your career value is being measured at all times. How differently would you react? Would you realize that what the coworker did was not personal and he may just not be good at what he does? Take the high road and show that you have substantial value. Provide the information he needs, then move on. By doing this, you display a positive aspect of your career value. And also, by changing the way that you operate in a stressful situation like this, you just moved your Æ.

You can use your Æ to justify raises and get new opportunities like jobs, projects, assignments, or leadership roles. You can build career momentum by documenting and promoting your Æ. By using the methods I describe in this book and the companion website, you can

Dream Big, Get Stuff Done and Have Fun!

You now have a plan to survive in an automated world, through activities that will allow you to learn, reinvent yourself, and add higher value to your career. Trust is the center of your Æ, as you need to believe that your job has value and can be improved. You also have to be willing to take the small steps to move your Æ, or you will be left behind.

To add to your career value:

- Don't wait for permission
- Don't ask for permission
- Take Control

Knowing, growing and showing your career Æ will allow you and others to fully understand the results of the value that you have brought to the table. If you don't understand it yourself, you will not be able to help others understand your value, and miss out on some excellent career opportunities. The next section of this book will cover ways to grow your Æ.

Chapter Debrief

- Your career Æ requires regular engagement from you

- Know your audience when describing your Æ, as it is their interpretation of the value that matters

- Your attitude and how you react in situations have direct impacts to your Æ

Your Turn

1. Think of one situation where you reacted quickly. Write two phrases to describe how you would handle it now, after reading this chapter.

2. Describe the last time that you waited for permission to do something. Would you be willing to just do it next time, and why?

Part 2

Grow Your Career Value

MOVE YOUR Æ

10

Plan Your Æ

The future depends on what you do today.

—Mahatma Gandhi

I remember when my 5-year-old daughter and I were leaving the house one day, and she pointed down the street and said, "Daddy, what is that?" I looked down the street and did not see anything, so I responded to her that I did not know what she was pointing at, which is when she bounded down the sidewalk right up to the red fire hydrant about 10 feet from our property line. "What's this?" she asked.

As I explained to her what fire hydrants are for, I found it peculiar that I knew it was there but had not paid attention to it any longer. In fact, since we had a short driveway and no garage, I had to park my vehicle on the street, positioning it very carefully between that hydrant and our mailbox, as each of them has no-parking zones around them. So, I was aware of the hydrant each day but did not pay attention to it. How can that happen?

It is similar to the 2-picture puzzle I described in the introduction where we focus so much on the big picture that we lose focus of all of the details. Have you ever tried to stare at the road directly in front of you when you are on a bicycle or driving a car? Be careful. As you quickly find out, you have a chance of not only careening off course but running head-first into objects in your path if you are not looking up and focusing on the big picture. It is necessary for us to see beyond many of the tiny details so that we can stay focused on our current task.

But when it comes to your career, you have to unlearn this process. It is crucial that you can document the small things that lead to the big picture or you will find yourself stuck in a pothole. Do you have a career strategic plan? Probably not, and nor did I decades ago. I know it sounds complicated, but let me help you get started.

First, what do you want to do for a career? Write down the big picture. It doesn't mean that you are going to get there right away, but the ultimate goal is to reach it. Make it something realistic that fits within your space, which means that with additional skills, training or education, you can reach it.

At my age (51), height (6' 2") and body build (think Dad Bod gone wild), I will not be an Olympic swimmer or jockey on a horse in the Kentucky Derby. But, I have always known that I love to write, speak and help people improve their abilities. So, my strategic plan for about seven years now has been to become a professional author and speaker. I have set goals along the way to get me to this point, and I know that you can, too. The key is to start small, set a vision, create achievable goals to get the small wins, monitor your progress and earn rewards.

Organizations who win awards for being best places to work have created effective ways to train and develop their employees. One of the strategies is to help the employees put together a plan for development, called the Individual Development Plan, or IDP. The IDP is a tool to assist you in your career and personal development by documenting your professional goals and strengths, then using that information to develop a list of activities that will support your development needs. Its primary purpose is to:

- Help you reach short and long-term career goals
- Improve your performance at your current job

To be most effective, you must assume personal responsibility and accountability for taking the initiative for your professional development by acquiring or enhancing the skills you need to stay current in your job. The IDP can include the activities in which you will obtain additional skills and experience, such as:

- Classroom training
- Online training and webinars
- Professional seminars and conferences
- Job rotation opportunities
- Job shadowing
- Apprenticeship or on-the-job training
- Self-study programs
- Mentoring programs
- Personality and aptitude assessments

A solid plan will help you leverage your strengths and talents while providing you with new knowledge and experience that will help you achieve higher levels of performance at your job[35]. By developing an IDP, you learn how to leverage your expertise into a satisfying and productive career. Done correctly, this will also put you on the radar of the organization's leaders, and can easily put you in a more powerful position for promotional opportunities.

Companies are beginning to recruit from non-traditional channels to find workers who have the agility to take their skills and experience from one job, industry or profession, and use them effectively in another. You must be able to document your career value so that you show agility to learn and grow, which will get you access to new opportunities.

These leaders are also trying to figure out "potential," and your Æ will help show it. More than just a list of credentials, your Æ provides you with a new credential of career achievement. You can demonstrate your capacity to learn, grow and succeed in ways that they are not considering. You want a way to do this more quickly and efficiently, as the recruiter only has so much time. The easier you make her job, the more quickly she will talk with you about the opportunities she has available.

As you develop a framework for your career plan, it is time to focus on the goals. One common acronym used to capture the best attributes for goals is "SMART," which stands for:

- Specific
- Measurable
- Achievable
- Relevant
- Time-bound[36]

This term was first used in a paper by George T. Doran that appeared in *Management Review*[37]. To see how this "smart" abbreviation will help you stay on track with your goals, let's take an example goal and validate that it meets our criteria.

Sample Goal

Before my next annual performance review, I will attend at least four webinars or in-person seminars regarding the topic of Talent Acquisition to keep updated on best practices in the field.

Specific

Find the details. Like a good detective, you ask the "who, what, where, when and why" questions for your goal. What action am I going to take? Who might be involved? Where will the work be done? The toughest part of SMART is knowing how much detail is too little, how much is too much, and like Goldilocks, find out how much is just right. Start with at least two items from the "who, what, where" combination. You will get better at the specific details that work best for you as you practice using this method.

In our sample goal, the specific details are:

- Before my next annual performance review (when)
- I will take action (who)
- Attend at least four events (what)
- Events are webinars or in-person seminars (where)
- Topic of events is "Talent Acquisition" (what)
- Keep updated on best practices (why)

As you can see, those are precise descriptions that cover all of the questions. Again, selecting just two specific details is a good place to start.

Measurable

There is a common phrase that says, "You cannot improve something if you cannot measure it." That does not mean that something cannot get better unless it is measured. Instead, it implies that if you want to show that an action you took had an impact, you need to start with a baseline measurement, take your action, then measure again. You will find that there was no change or that the activity had a positive or negative impact from the original baseline.

In our sample goal, the measurable items are:

- Before my next annual performance review
- Attend at least four events

Assuming that I have ten months until my next annual performance review, I set today as my baseline. Since in the past few minutes I have not attended a webinar or seminar, I am starting at zero. By the end of 10 months, I can count how many events I have attended. That makes it easy for me to measure with simple math.

Achievable

We are capable of setting any goal, including lofty ones. At the beginning of my career, I had planned to retire by age 30. As I got close to that age, I realized that this was not a SMART goal for many reasons, including the fact that I did not include any measurements for "retirement" and that I had been married for five years and now had two children under the age of three. I would say that my goal when I left college was not achievable, given the other priorities I had set for my life.

For our sample goal, we consider the following attributes for achievability:

- Before my next annual performance review
- Attend at least four events
- Events are webinars or in-person seminars

We will start at the bottom: can I attend webinars or in-person seminars? Yes, I have the means to be able to do that at work or in my spare time at night or weekends. Can I attend at least 4 of them? Combining this question with the first attribute, where I know that I have ten months, I believe I can achieve the goal of attending one of those events every 2.5 months. Final answer: Yes, this goal is achievable.

Relevant

The goal must be appropriate to your circumstances or applicable to where you want to go in your career or any other part of your life. This one is the loosest of the attributes, as the goal can be directly related to your current job or a future career that you are investigating. In developing your career goals, relevancy has the most significant impact when you consider if achieving this goal will keep you ahead of the fast-changing workplace.

In other words, if by the time you achieve the goal, your skills are outdated or you are at a significant disadvantage because of the resources you expended to reach the goal, you need to question if the goal is an appropriate one to go after. Students who take on large sums of student debt to achieve college degrees sometimes find that the debt put them at a disadvantage in the marketplace by limiting their job and mobility options.

For our sample goal, the relevancy centers around:

- Topic of events is "Talent Acquisition."
- Keep updated on best practices

Since I have a passion for helping people connect with and find their best opportunities, continuing to keep updated on best practices in the Talent Acquisition field is very relevant and not likely to hinder my opportunities in the future.

Time-bound

Finally, we come to the concept of time. While we cannot create time, we can use it as a marker for our goals. Time-bound goals should have a beginning and an end, or they can be open-ended, with specific actions taken at intervals specified within the goal.

For instance, if an open-ended SMART goal says that you will "provide monthly updates to the governance committee," the activity meets the time criteria, even though there is no end date. You bind each set of updates to the monthly governance committee meeting time.

In our sample goal, time is indicated by:

- Before my next annual performance review

I stated that I have an annual performance review, so it occurs every 12 months. Using our example, I indicated that I had ten months remaining. By making the statement that I will achieve this goal by that next review, I have created the boundary of ten months in which to complete the tasks.

Creating a plan and setting goals is one of the most challenging parts of developing your career. Because you are a unique combination of talents, skills, and experiences, no one can tell you what is best for you. It is a journey. But you don't have to take the journey alone. Setting goals helps you develop the path and get to your destination. You need the help of others, so surround yourself with people who care about you and can help coach and mentor you.

Stay focused on the tasks. Know what you need to accomplish to get what you want out of life. Know the target, such as the end zone in an American football game. Don't be distracted by the fans. It is 3rd and eight at your 40-yard line. Don't risk the throw of a "Hail Mary" pass. Get the 8 yards and stay alive for the next set of downs. As Lori Greiner says, is your play going to make you a "Hero or Zero?[38]" Don't be either. Stay with the plan to earn the 8 yards, because it gets you one step closer to your target. Getting there in one shot may make you a hero, but you will feel more accomplished when you incrementally move towards and then reach the ultimate goal.

Chapter Debrief

- Focus on the details, and document them, in order to grow your Æ

- Individual Development Plans (IDP) are a great way for you to manage your career.

- Surround yourself with coaches and mentors who will help you develop your abilities

Your Turn

1. Pick one goal you want to accomplish in the next six months and define it using the SMART goal technique.

2. Identify one coach and one mentor with whom you will build a relationship over the next three months.

11

Document Your Æ

Historical gap is created due to missing written records.

— Lailah Gifty Akita

Think about the top times in your career when you dreaded doing a task. While I am not a magician nor a mind reader, I bet with high certainty that I know two of those occurrences:

- You are providing input for your performance review
- You are putting together your resume to apply for another job

Was I right? As you nod your head, "Yes," I will explain why I had such a high level of certainty.

Believe it or not, even though I present with a high-level of confidence in understanding my value to the team and organization, I also do not look forward to these exercises. I particularly dread having to craft a resume for a specific job opportunity because I have a significant amount of information from the nearly 30 years of my adult working life from which to source the data for the resume. As I sort through the reams of data, it becomes overwhelming to figure out what to put into the short resume format. Luckily for you, I have figured out how to overcome this issue, and it is called documentation. Okay, I just said the next word that most people dread.

But stick with me through the end of the chapter, and I will prove to you:

1. Why documentation is so essential to promoting your career value

2. It is not as difficult as you think to document your value effectively

You will agree with me that many people, including you, tend to overlook their strengths and accomplishments. It is a natural side effect of humility. If we talk about how good we are at something or how successful we are, it sounds like bragging. On the opposite end of that argument, if you do not put together a list of what you are good at and what you have done, who else is going to do it?

Let's take a brief look at what it means to show your career value. I will cover this in depth in a later chapter, but for now, it is important for you to understand why promoting your value opens doors for you. Think of the last time that you learned about a product or service that you ended up buying. What was it about that product that attracted you to it? How did you learn about the product? Did you read any reviews and if so, who were the reviewers? And once you bought it, did it meet your expectations?

As you may have noticed, I was asking many questions that a marketing team will use to develop a marketing plan for a new product or service. One specific area that stands out in the situation above is the concept of content marketing. Content marketing is the practice of creating content, like advertisements, videos, social media posts, and blog articles that describe the concept behind your product or service in a way that will attract a specific audience. In fact, one of the easiest ways to get started with this is to create what are called "personas" of your customers.

A persona is a "stand-in" person who has attributes aligned with your target customers. For instance, if you are selling surfboards, you will most likely have characteristics of one of your personas be someone who lives near a body of water with continuous waves, who can swim and who has some athletic ability. By defining those specific attributes, you can now develop content targeting people in specific geographic areas and who engage in sport and athletic activities. Of course, it gets a lot more complicated than this, but this is a simple view to help you understand how content marketing applies to product promotion, which applies to your career in two ways:

1. You need to understand the type of career opportunities that you seek

2. You have to get your information in front of people who will be attracted to your career attributes

Whether you are interested in expanding your skills in your current profession or moving into another professional field, you have to develop a list of the skills, training, and credentials you will need to make a move. Similar to how a marketer develops personas with attributes related to their products, you will put together a list of attributes for a specific job. From there, you will match the list of your career attributes to find alignment. This map will now provide you with a plan to obtain more education, training or experience to fill in the gaps. As you read this book and follow the steps outlined, you will have such a map.

Once you have a career map developed, you next work on the types of people or organizations who will be interested in your career attributes and aspirations. This is also similar to the content marketers who now must find ways to get the attention of their target personas. Just as marketers use many creative ways to accomplish this goal, you can use techniques and your network of supporters to promote your value. Successful people get to where they are in their careers because they have developed their abilities to use their networks to promote their career value, and so can you.

We took a small side trip to discuss how promoting your career value will help you find more opportunities for success. Now, let's return to the point of this chapter, which is to document your value. From what we have seen, content promotion requires a list of attributes about the product and the target audience. It is the same for your career. You must learn how to create the catalog of attributes for both your career value and for the jobs you are targeting. With these lists, you will document how your skills, talents, education, experiences and so many other career attributes align with this catalog, which begins to shed light on your full career value.

What about your resume? Professionals say that you should have a different resume for each job to which you are applying. They also talk about incorporating relevant keywords, so the resume gets recognized. But you are more than a few pages and a dozen keywords. Your entire career is a complex set of experiences, talents, skills, jobs, accomplishments, failures and interactions with others. Each situation takes place in a different context. It is important for you to document what makes you successful in that context, using a tool like the Æ.

I had said earlier in this chapter that once I convinced you why documentation is vital to your career growth and promotion, I was going to explain why it is not as difficult as you think. To accomplish this goal, I will bring in the idea of a Memory Jar.

Did you, or someone you know, ever use a Memory Jar or Memory Box? The idea is simple and succinct: you acquire a jar or box and use it to store memories. I suggest decorating it by adding flair, maybe something that is out of sync with your household or office decor. While the adornment does not add to the ability to store memories, it does help to draw your attention at times so that you will remember to add a memory. As I wrote that last sentence, something seems odd about having to remember to record a memory. Be careful that you don't get into an endless memory loop following that advice.

Documenting your career value is as easy as dropping a memory into your career jar once in a while. If you prefer to do this electronically, you can start simply by creating a document in Excel, Word, or use the tools at PaulCarneyWorks.com. Or you can create a physical jar in which you drop small pieces of note paper. The format and technology do not matter. And don't worry about whether the detail you are providing on the note is too small. Set aside that decision-making process for later, when you are reviewing your notes, as it will get in the way of adding notes to your "jar."

As you hit your documentation stride, you will know what is just right for the details you need. After you have been dropping notes in your career jar for a few weeks, you can develop more structure, such as at the end of each week, look back at your calendar and the work you have done, then drop a few notes in there. Once you do this for a few months, you will see how quickly the notes add up and when you go back through them, you will easily remember something you did that added value to your development, your work, and your career. Without the documentation, you are bound to forget, and if you don't remember it, you cannot promote it.

Chapter Debrief

- Documenting the activities that identify your career value is essential, and not difficult to do

- Use techniques like content marketing to identify the stories that you want to tell so that you can document and store the details you need

- Identify the next place you want to be and map your journey to get there

Your Turn

1. Pick one concept for which you want to be recognized within the next six months, then put together the five details you will need to collect to tell the story. Then do it.

2. Identify a new skill or profession that you want to aim for, then create a catalog of at least five skills that are needed to achieve it. Compare that list to what you already have, and fill in the gaps with development opportunities.

12

Strengthen Your Æ

You can't use up creativity.

The more you use, the more you have.

— Maya Angelou

When I ask you the following question, capture the first thought that arrives in your mind:

**If you could improve one thing about you,
what would it be?**

The odds are very high that you chose something that you are not particularly good at or is a nagging nuisance like losing weight or eating less junk food. We have spent our lives being asked, or even coerced, to focus on fixing things that are wrong with us. As we identify the catalog of weaknesses, we develop a list of the actions that we will take to fix or improve our shortcomings. Even worse, there is no shortage of people who are willing to provide their advice and guidance on the corrective actions that would help us improve.

What if, instead, you focused on your potentiality? Wouldn't that be more fun?

It turns out that you should focus on adding to your strengths and being happy while you do it. Shawn Achor[39] has one of the most-watched TED talk videos in which he talks about the power of "happiness." His story of how he convinces his young sister that she is a unicorn is worth hearing. Shawn then goes on to describe the research that shows how using positive thoughts cause your brain to be more productive, and how you can train your brain to become more positive.

Lauren C. Howe Ph.D.[40], wrote an interesting article entitled, "A Self-Improvement Secret: Work on Strengths[41]," where she describes research showing that people believe that they can change their weaknesses more than they can change their strengths. She makes the case that we could be approaching self-improvement from the wrong angle by believing that our weaknesses are more changeable than our strengths. Dr. Howe then goes on to state:

> Neglecting the practice of strengths – failing to work on the good things that we already have – could overlook a source of happiness. In fact, programs designed to "train your strengths" can have benefits.

Given how the power of positive brain activity can make you more productive, and that focusing on your strengths can build your happiness while you improve, I recommend the following activity:

1. Make a list of abilities in which you believe you have

strengths

2. Choose one that you want to improve

3. Make a plan to do it

From my own experiences and the research I have read, the positive effects of this improvement will build your confidence to take on other abilities that you want to strengthen. Eventually, you have the power to take on something that you are not good at and want to improve and will have the confidence to do it. Learning how to strengthen your body and mind is directly tied to your career success.

Athletes use strength training and conditioning to improve their agility, speed, strength, balance, and endurance. They typically follow high-intensity workouts where they use body weight and resistance training to strengthen their muscles. They include aerobic drills into their workout routines to enhance the capacity and endurance of their cardio and respiratory systems. By doing this, they are ready to face the demands of high-intensity sports, especially at the professional level.

The athletes balance many different types of programs using short, intensive intervals to keep their bodies challenged. Athletes also incorporate nutrition programs into their training. Led by nutrition experts, the athletes will eat prescribed foods and supplements at specific intervals throughout the day. These regiments allow the athletes to condition their bodies for their training exercises and the performance of a match or game. Combining strength, nutrition and proper rest periods, athletes continue to push the limits of the human body as they compete.

Don't worry; I am not advocating that you have to use weights and run five miles a day to keep your career in shape. Instead, you can use techniques that are similar to athletes to keep your career fit, ready to respond to the challenges it will face. I suggest a simple template that you can use to manage your Æ training and conditioning that allows you to jot down brief notes to keep track of your results. As you can see, this is where you can realize the value of the previous chapter on "Document Your Æ." You can find copies of all templates and a web-based documentation tool at the companion website of this book, PaulCarneyWorks.com.

Here is one example from the web site:

Date	Events I Expected	Events I Did Not Expect

For a given date, jot down brief phrases that describe expected events in your day. Like attending a team meeting where you discussed the upcoming deadlines, having a 1:1 meeting with your boss where you asked for assistance on a project and the one hour of planned maintenance time when the computer system you were using was not available for you to complete your work.

In the second column, "Events I Did Not Expect," record the "extra" things that occur in your day. These are the items that can directly impact not only your efficiency but your Æ if you are not careful. That is why it is important to record these events so that you have them as a reference at a later date when you are compiling input for your performance review or putting together a resume for a new opportunity. If you do not record them now, you will likely not remember them later. Ask anyone around you if they can remember the top two items that affected their work six months ago and most will not be able to recall much. If they had recorded the events, they can quickly refresh their memory and produce the moment of clarification, "Ah, that's right, we had the client call that day, and they completely changed the requirements for the project that we had been working on for two weeks."

As you start, I strongly suggest that you commit yourself to recording at least three of these entries per work week. You can pick a day of the week that works best, perhaps a Thursday so that Monday is not so far away and you have completed four of the five days of the standard workweek. Whatever the term, make a promise to yourself to stick to the plan and create the entry.

Ignore the advice from your grammar and writing teachers. Do not use complete sentences. Use phrases, bullets, draw lines, or whatever suits your style to get the information recorded quickly. I suggest that you log only 2-3 phrases at a time so that you do not feel overwhelmed. As you write, be sure to include enough detail to help spur a memory later, even possibly a year later. For some people like me, a few words will help me recall the entire event. As a teacher and leader, I have learned during the past three decades that most people need to record more details, like names, places or even decisions made by a team, to paint the full picture of the event. Over time, you will become more comfortable with the level of detail that works best for you.

I know that after trying this for about two months, I looked forward to jotting down my ideas and not only did it become a daily routine, but I was adding more depth where I knew that I would rely on this information later to help me remember what I did to strengthen my Æ. Top performers know how to focus on their strengths to their advantage. By using these techniques to enhance your Æ, you will move towards the top of the heap, which is fantastic because the view is better from up there.

As you strengthen your Æ, you will need to understand how to use its power to move ahead of the competition. Having strength and not using it to your advantage is a waste of your resources. Figuring out how to leverage strength into power is a tricky feat. Since power can amplify your speed and send you quickly down your career path, let's take a look at power and how you can effectively use it.

You gain power not through title or position, but through your ability to earn respect from others and to influence their thoughts and behaviors. Think of some of the go-to people you know at your company or in your community. Are they always the top leaders? Most likely not. So, what characteristics do these people have that allow them to be successful at influencing others? When I ask this during my "Networking 101" presentations, there is typically an extensive list generated by the audience, including:

- Outgoing
- Charismatic
- Good listeners
- Good speakers
- Driven
- Extensive network of people they know
- Remember people's names and other details
- Have a positive attitude, cheerfulness about them

- Ask questions about others
- Get excited about events and results
- Smile often
- Good storytellers
- Well-read, up-to-date on latest topics
- Involved in many groups

I then ask the most critical question of the session, "How many people do you know exhibit ALL of these qualities, ALL of the time?" So far, I have not had anyone identify the Super Hero who meets the criteria. That is because each of us brings our qualities to our relationships and you do not have to be all of those at one time to be successful.

Guess what? You have some of these qualities, too. You are not fully aware of them and your impact on the people around you when you use them. Beyond that, you need to promote that impact, so others see your value, which leads to influence and persuasion. It is not magic. You offer a lot of value to the people around you, and you would not be reading this book and following the lessons if you did not believe that you can improve your ability to add more value.

The best way to get started is to focus on one or two that you want to be good at and strengthen the skills you already have. No matter where you start and which skill you pick to strengthen, I will state that to be most influential, you have to have confidence, empathy and a willingness to fail.

The test of your strength is when you face adversity. It is easy to get along and manage decisions when everything is going well, and the path is clear. But when things are not going the way you planned, obstacles begin to appear on the road, and your vision is murky. That is when you understand why you do what you do. Facing significant events in your life, especially life-altering ones, will force you into this mode. Don't wait for that to happen. Determine who you are today and why you do what you do. At that point, you are prepared when adversity shows up at your doorstep.

Chapter Debrief

-   Improve your Æ by focusing on your strengths

-   Follow techniques similar to the training and conditioning that athletes use for peak performance

-   Top performers commit to increasing their value and use it to their advantage

Your Turn

1. Pick two items from the list of attributes of successful people earlier in this chapter and write down how you will improve your ability to be recognized for those attributes.

2. Write down the exact plan (daily, weekly, which days, time of day, etc.) and use the paper or electronic tools to record your activities, thoughts and ideas. Commit to follow that plan for three months.

13

Develop Your Æ

None of us can change our yesterdays,
but all of us can change our tomorrows.

— Colin Powell

Historically, people survived by relying on generalized skills. For example, the farmer had to be a laborer, mechanic, animal doctor, and purveyor of many other skills to feed the family. As towns grew, people began to develop specialized skills to provide necessary services and earn money. With those specializations came professions like doctors, veterinarians, blacksmith, and bankers. And with these professions came the need for advanced education and skill development through higher education institutions and apprenticeships.

Over the past three decades, we have seen how computers and information systems have changed how we work. The explosive use of the internet has also had a direct impact on our employment. Jobs are requiring more specialized skills today. Read any job posting and see the litany of skills that they desire. In the talent acquisition industry, we call it "looking for the rainbow unicorn" or the "purple squirrel."

As organizations become so specific in their requirements, how do you know if you match up? In reality, most companies need people with aptitude and the attitude to want to learn and grow, along with analysis and problem-solving skills. If they can find that person, like you, they can teach you the skills they need.

Does your company focus on the "high performers?" Who is a "high performer?" What characteristics do a high-performing employee have? Do you have some of those qualities? Why doesn't your boss recognize their value? It is likely that your company hasn't tracked it, which is why you need to start documenting and developing your Æ.

In his book *Chasing Stars: The Myth of Talent and the Portability of Performance*[42], Harvard professor Boris Groysberg states that "...the question of whether human capital is primarily generalizable or firm-specific is debated as if there were only two possible answers." He is referring to the fact that it is not merely a yes/no question, which is where the Æ comes in. It is more than just a set of skills and credentials. It is the whole set of characteristics that make up your career and its value. In his book, he states that the company and its resources play a significant role in your success. If this is true, it is even more vital for you to develop your career value so that it is portable to other jobs, professions or companies.

The entire value proposition from your unique collection of competencies, skills, talents, education, and experience is only as good as the direct impact it has on driving business results. The means of how you got there is more than the results. But the context of your value is being based on only the results, unless your performance, inputs, and impact on the work that was done are documented, qualified, and transparent to others for use in furthering your career opportunities.

Many people confuse the list of efforts that they make toward creating business results as enough proof of their value. But that is dead wrong and here is why: at the point that you stop producing results or the value of your results is less than the compensation you are receiving, you will find yourself looking for a new job.

Don't believe that trying to do something and documenting all of the great things that you tried are going to keep you employed. Your organization is compensating you to add value to business results that your efforts produce. No results mean no return for the organization's investment in your time and talent, and at some point, they are going to make the tough decision to find another resource.

As you develop your Æ, view time as a resource and not a barrier. You and your team do not fail because you lack time to finish the tasks, you miss achievement because you did not properly allocate and use the time to your advantage. By developing your Æ, you learn how to integrate time with the skills, abilities, talents, education, and knowledge of you and your team members to create value. The better you understand and develop your abilities, the more effective you become at using them to create value.

One fundamental rule that all successful people follow has to do with time:

**Successful people allocate time each week
for their development.**

Just as we discussed earlier in the book how athletes use their time to strengthen themselves through training and conditioning, you have to allocate time for your career development. Do not rely on your boss or your organization to do this for you. If they do lend support in your efforts, then you are fortunate to have their support. But in the end, your career development is your responsibility, and you need to take the steps now to manage it.

How much time is the right amount to spend each week? The answer depends on your goals, your work schedule and more importantly, if others, like children or elderly parents, rely on you for their caring and support. As my children were growing up, my wife developed a system that allocated daily "screen time" for the kids. She had read articles, and we discussed what we thought was appropriate, then she created a formula that incorporated their age as a variable:

Daily Screen Time Minutes = Age * 10

"Screen time" was for computers and video games in the late 1990s and early 2000s, so the internet was less of a factor than it is today, and there were no mobile devices with apps. In those days, most of the computer time was spent on software loaded onto the computer. And television counted separately, as they were allowed to watch an educational show when they got home from school.

In this case, the basic premise was to limit the time spent on activities like computer and video games. And this type of formula can be used to calculate the minimum number of hours you should spend on your career development each week. As an example, what if you used a formula like this:

Weekly Career Development Hours = (65 - your age) / 8

According to my simple formula, if you are 25 years old, then you should spend a **minimum** of (65 - 25)/8 or 5 hours a week on your career development. Similarly, if you are 45, you should spend a **minimum** of (65 - 45)/8 or 2.5 hours a week. Develop the formula that makes sense for you and your situation. The important part is that you develop a formula and track your time each week so that you do not fall behind in your career.

How you spend that time can vary from week to week and topic to topic. Not all of the time needs to be formal time, spent in a classroom or completing online courses. There are a variety of ways that you can learn each week, including:

- Reading and responding to articles (magazine, blogs, LinkedIn)
- Watching topical videos (LinkedIn Learning, YouTube, TED talks)
- Reviewing research papers (universities, scientific or professional journals)
- Conducting data analysis (download data files, look for connections and patterns)

The list provided is a small example of ways you can vary the learning you do so that it is more enjoyable. I also recommend that you branch out from what you typically follow and find people whose thoughts and ideas do not directly align with you. I have found that by trying to understand why they think the way they do, it helps me understand how I arrive at my point of view. By using this method, I have changed my point of view at times after learning from the other people.

———

In developing your career Æ, there is a distinct difference between making a decision and making a choice. When you make a choice, you are selecting from various options and can typically modify your option if more information becomes available. The main characteristics of making a choice are:

- You make choices many times each day
- They require minimal information processing and thought
- They have fewer consequences to your career

In your daily life, you make choices about what to wear, where you are going to eat and who you could call to hang out with after work. The difference between if you get a sandwich or order take out for lunch will typically not have lasting effects on your life. And if you are not happy after making one choice, you can always choose a different option next time.

Decisions, on the other hand, are like casting your vote in an election. Once you make the decision, it is not easy to go back and change your vote. The main characteristics of making a decision are:

- They carry more weight and are done less frequently
- They require more information and processing power, and typically more time
- They will affect the path of your career

A decision to buy a home or get married to a specific person will have a direct effect on your life. In your career, you make decisions to stay with a job or find another one, to pursue a specific degree or to position yourself for a promotion. A decision requires more time and thought since it can take years to move to another career track or pay the debt you might have to assume to earn a degree.

It is essential to understand when you are making more of a decision than a choice. The strongest of decisions may send you down a path that you did not expect, but rarely does it put you into a position from which you cannot pivot into another direction. Part of learning how to develop your career involves knowing when you need to spend more time and conduct more research into a decision, but not get so hamstrung by this process that you cannot make choices in your career.

In my experience, no matter what path you choose and decisions you make in your career, two significant characteristics will allow you to develop to your fullest potential. You do not want to spend a lot of resources, like your time, talent and cash, if you do not have a solid foundation of the two principles of self-regard and professionalism.

Self-regard has to do with how you evaluate yourself in a professional setting. It allows you to understand how co-workers perceive you through your actions and words. People with high self-regard:

- Take responsibility for their decisions
- Hold themselves accountable for their actions
- Exhibit a positive attitude
- Are proactive learners

The people you see around you who have high self-regard accept when they make decisions, even if the results are not what they expected. They are open to ideas and work to reduce assumptions that they may have about people or situations. While it is difficult to do, you need to carefully evaluate and share any assumptions you are making when you deal with people to make sure that you have not overlooked a detail that matters.

Exhibiting a positive attitude does not mean that they see the bright side of every situation nor are they the cheerleaders who consistently work to drive up the spirit of the crowd. You may see them get a little more focused when the challenges become tougher. But overall, they will keep a positive outlook on the situation and bring together the resources needed to move ahead.

Not only do they proactively seek learning opportunities, but they also learn vicariously through other people's learning experiences, which is an attribute that I developed early in life and have used extensively to build my career value. While I may not have directly experienced a learning opportunity, I can learn how another person dealt with a situation and observe the results.

I remember early in my career when I was a software developer. We had a manager who had less tolerance for the younger developers, like me, who would question why we were going down one path when it seemed more efficient to develop the software using another method. I had learned how to effectively make my point without drawing his ire, but one person, in particular, I will refer to him as Jim, did not understand this concept.

The manager did not overreact, until one day when it seemed too much for him to hold back. Instead of calling Jim into his office to explain his dislike for the process, and then working with Jim to help him understand how to make his point more effectively, the manager publicly berated Jim. Not only did this create a bad scene for the manager, but Jim was devastated.

Most people would have learned just from Jim's example and not want to become the target of such actions. In fact, many people would just have "learned" to not challenge the manager. But I learned more. Beyond already having learned how to effectively work with the manager to persuade him to my point of view, I learned that when I would become a manager someday, I would not use a public scolding as a development technique.

I could see the devastation in Jim's eyes as I realized that he did not fully understand why he was receiving this feedback in such a harsh way. I processed the situation from the manager's standpoint and also realized that he had not fully understood what he had done to Jim that day. While I had not experienced the specific situation as a manager, I learned vicariously through my manager's experience. By developing the techniques to do this, you can turn every situation at work into a learning lesson for you. And be sure to document it.

The other characteristic that will affect your ability to develop your career is professionalism. In summary, professionalism is defined by:

- Work habits
- Interpersonal communication
- Meeting deadlines and following through

Work habits reflect how well you can work independently or as part of a team, as your career will depend on you being able to do both effectively. Your reliability to arrive at work ready to complete the tasks required to do your job is another measure of your work habits. When you are on a team, what roles you typically take and how well you get along with people are also included when others will describe the strength of your work habits.

Interpersonal communication has multiple dimensions. On the one side, it has to do with how well you can express a concept or make a request using written communications, like emails or instant messages. It also it includes your ability to present your ideas in person in both informal meetings and during formal presentations. These are both skills that you should consistently develop, as I have seen many intelligent, capable people who have not risen in their careers to the point for which they aim simply because they could not express themselves in writing or speech.

There are multiple ways that you can develop your written skills. You can take online courses that will teach you methods for effective writing. They will teach you how to build an outline of your idea, then construct the document using an introduction, followed by your supporting paragraphs and then your conclusion and call-to-action, if there is one. But you can also develop your writing skills in less formal ways, like following conversations on a blog or social media sites like LinkedIn and adding your thoughts and ideas. These discussions show you how other people state their opinions in productive ways and allow you to experiment on methods of persuading others as you learn.

Conducting oral presentations is one area that causes dread for most people. The National Institute of Mental Health indicates that public speaking anxiety affects about

73% of the U.S. population[43]. According to Statistic Brain, more people are afraid of glossophobia, which is the scientific term for public speaking anxiety, than fear death (68%), spiders (30.5%), darkness (11%) and heights (10%)[44]. The odds tell me that you are most likely in that 73%.

Healthy development of your career involves improving your ability to conduct an effective presentation. I am not advocating that you speak at a conference in front of 1,000 people, but at many points in your career, you will be called upon to present an idea or update to a group of people, and you need to focus on developing this skill to move your Æ.

One of the best ways to learn practical presentation skills is just to do it. I suggest you find a workshop in your local area where you can learn the techniques and practice them. Part of the practice includes recording your presentation so that you can review it later to determine performance weaknesses. Joining a club like Toastmasters is also a beneficial way to learn and grow in a very supportive setting. I earned my Competent Communicator designation from my local Toastmasters club, and even though I started with a lot of experience and talent around doing speeches at conferences and in classrooms, I learned many techniques to improve my skills. I know that you can, too.

Finally, meeting deadlines and following through on your actions is an integral part of your professional career. Each of us finds ways to manage our schedules and complete our work. You may find that detailed lists help you meet goals. Others do daily check-ups on their tasks so that they know what to focus on that day. No matter the methods you use, your career development will rely on how well you can get things done.

Developing your Æ allows you to align your strengths and needs with those of the organization. If they do not match in your current situation, then create a plan to develop your skills by focusing on what is needed. If the alignment gap between what you offer and what the company needs is wide, you may need to find an organization or another job where they are more closely aligned to be most effective in your career.

It is your responsibility to become a master of your career value. By developing your value, you create more choices and opportunities for your career, including ones that would not have been possible without your awareness and ability to develop your Æ. It does not matter where you start, but that you get started now and document along the way.

Chapter Debrief

- Companies need people with aptitude and the attitude to want to learn and grow, along with analysis and problem-solving skills
- Your Æ value is not based on a list of activities, but instead on the impact you have on business results
- Understand when you are making a decision or a choice
- The two significant characteristics for potential are self-regard and professionalism

Your Turn

1. Determine the minimum number of weekly career development hours to which you will commit and create the list of activities for next week to reach those hours.

2. Write down three examples each of how you exhibit self-regard and professionalism.

14

Network Your Æ

You can make more friends in two months by becoming interested in other people than you can in two years by trying to get other people interested in you.

— Dale Carnegie

When I launched my first start-up company, I had a plan. Yes, you need to have a plan to get to where you want to go. One of the toughest jobs leading a start-up organization is to know when you need to flex your plan, or as it was called in the day when to "pivot." Which means that you recognize either your plan is taking you down a road you did not want to go down, or an opportunity that you did not anticipate has suddenly moved to the top of the list. In either case, recognizing, and making a move is very tough.

The same is true as you build your network of support, which you need to be successful in any part of your life. Whether it is your family, your friends, your co-workers or community, it is crucial that you have built a network of people who trust you and will provide support for you as you face life's obstacles. Each successful person can point to numerous people who helped her along her path of successes.

How do you calculate the value of a network? It would be the summation of the distinction each person brings to their groups. As you can imagine, the broader your network, the faster the value accumulates. Can you calculate the full merit of those connections? Most likely not. You know that if you invest $100 in the stock market and get a 5% annual rate of return, you have $105 at the end of the year. But without a formula, why should you invest in building your network if you do not know what return you will get?

I cannot answer definitively what value you will derive from your network or if you will get a return that you believe is worth the investment. But I can say that just like the stock market there is one truism:

If you invest 0, you will get a 0 return.

Switch your thinking so that you build your network as a way to help people, instead of looking for a return, and you will find the value for your investment. Over time, you will discover connections that will help you find opportunities, some of them when you are not even looking. Remember that is what some people call "lucky," but you know that it is because you were prepared to recognize and mobilize when the opportunity was available to move ahead in your career.

I know this because I am a person who creates opportunities for the people in my network. Through my various online and offline networks, I help people not only get in front of hiring managers for job opportunities, I also connect them with others in my network to increase the odds of them finding the right position at the right company.

Numerous people tell others that I connected with them through LinkedIn and that I was the only one that responded to them out of dozens of requests that they sent.

I do not expect anything from answering these requests. Do I get something out of it? You bet. I get a great feeling because I helped someone, and hope that someone will do that for me in the future. I also get a few new friendships that have lasted many years later. You can do the same. It does not take a monetary investment from you nor does it require you to attend two business networking events and conferences a week. Instead, be a resource to people. Be active in social networks like LinkedIn by answering people's questions. If you read something of high interest, not only share it with your network but offer 1-2 sentences of why you found it interesting. You will see your network grow quickly if you engage with others.

By doing this throughout my career, I have had the good fortune of connecting with and working with some fantastic people. In fact, I have a group of people who have followed me from job to job and company to company. I did not plan for this to happen. It happened because I respond to people when they ask for assistance, and I am a resource with whom they enjoy working.

My father was a master at building a network in which he was the "hub" to an extensive group of people from all areas of life. Whenever he needed something, there was always a connection that was willing to help. And when they came to him, they knew that if he didn't have the direct ability to help, he would make contact with someone in his network who could assist the person. He taught me the power you have when you give often and ask as needed. He understood that the people in his network were glad to help him because it made them feel valuable, so he was not afraid to ask and neither should you.

When you build your Æ and create a strong network, your next job will come from one of those contacts. It is so much easier to get a job through networking than it is to answer job postings, no matter what skills and experience you have. Referrals directly from your network are the best. But to help the people in your network, they must know your career value. Most of them will know a piece of your worth. Your profiles on social media sites like LinkedIn will also provide another view of your career value, but their formats do not allow for full disclosure, just job titles, education, certifications and endorsements for skills. Your Æ is so much more than that, and you want everyone in your network to know your Æ so that they can connect you with the best opportunities.

Plus, wouldn't it be fun to work at a company where you know people? I know it is because I have done it many times in my career. In fact, there are quite a few people with whom I have worked at different companies. Even within large companies, I have worked with and managed multiple people across different departments. The power of your network is on display when you have colleagues who want to follow you to other groups.

Make connections and surround yourself with people who support you, not toxic people that drag you down. Be optimistic. That doesn't mean that you go around thinking everything is great. There are times that things downright stink and nothing seems to be going your way. But stop, take a breath, and realize that by being able to stand there, safely, and take a breath, things are not that bad. There are much worse situations to be in, you have gotten yourself through tougher times and then move onto the next step on your plan to move past this moment and find the one that holds value in you reaching your goals.

Chapter Debrief

- Focus on building a strong network, not just a large one

- Be a resource to others, and they will be strong advocates for you

- To tap the full capacity of your network, educate them about the many dimensions of your Æ

Your Turn

1. Discover three new people this month, either through social media or in your community, and have at least one conversation with each of them to find out what you can do to help them.

   a. BONUS: If they have access to resources you need, ask for help or to make a connection.

2. Once you have developed the first phase of your Æ, pick ten people in your network and share it with them to get their feedback. Be sure to document their input.

15

Motivate Your Æ

The question isn't who is going to let me;

it's who is going to stop me.

— Ayn Rand

Earning a promotion in your current job or company requires you to prove that you will add more value than you currently do. One phrase that typically ranks the lowest during most engagement surveys I have seen is that "promotions go to those who best deserve them." To understand why this is not a surprise, let's look at a quick example.

Ten people (six current employees, four from outside of the company) apply for a new job opening on your team that you have been waiting to fill. You believe that your five years on the team means that you know how the systems work, who the people are and you know how to get things done. Also, you received good performance reviews during this entire time. The new job requires skills that you have from another company at which you worked, but you have not had the opportunity to use them at this company yet.

Four people are selected for an interview, and you are not one of them. You don't understand why and you go to your boss and ask her. She states that you don't have the experience needed. You respond, "But I did something very similar at my previous job." She may then say that it was not clear on your resume. You know that you had so many items that you could put on your resume, but you parsed it down to just the items that you thought were necessary. And after review, you see that you did have an item on your resume that discussed that experience.

Is this a resume problem? Or, is the issue that your boss just doesn't understand or did not take adequate time to review your resume? In any case, it doesn't matter. The real issue is this:

You failed to promote your entire career value for the job.

Plain and simple. To be at the top of the list, you have to be able to show your value in ways that the other person will not only understand but appreciate and want. Assuming that you had a clear understanding of what the job required and what the boss was looking for in a person to fill that role and that you believe you are fully qualified, then you did not promote your value correctly. The process of determining your Æ will help you do this better.

There is another key phrase above regarding this job opportunity. While you may have understood the job requirements, did you fully understand what type of person the boss wanted to fill that role? As someone who has hired dozens of people directly in my career, and managed teams of recruiters that processed thousands of hires a year, I can say that each time a position opens, the manager is most likely looking for a different type of person to fill that role. This is why when colleagues approached me about their frustration with applying for internal jobs and not getting hired, I would make sure they understood to apply again if another similar role opens, even if it is on the same team. Because each time a manager is filling a position, he may be looking for a different type of person.

For example, if it is a team of seven analysts, and a job opening occurs, the manager will use many of this criteria to determine who they want to hire:

- What skills did the previous person bring to the team which will now be missing?
- What skills are needed for future work, which may be different from the current work?
- What additional technical, business or professional talents do we need to strengthen the team?

Once you know the answers to those questions, you can more readily evaluate if you have what is needed. How do you know the answers to these questions? You should ask the manager or recruiter before applying. If they have done their preparation, they will have direct answers to these questions.

One other possible scenario that plays out in the job scene is when you are told by a manager that you are not getting an interview because you lack the experience needed. Your knee-jerk reaction is most likely to ask, "How do I get the experience if I am not given the opportunity?" And that is the crux of the situation. You should not be relying on the company to give you the chance to develop that experience. Some great companies have development systems in place to help build their employee's talents and skills, but even in those cases, it is up to you to drive your progress.

There are multiple ways that you can gain the experience. You can volunteer to help in areas of the company that need an extra hand so that you can learn. You can talk with colleagues at lunch or over coffee to learn more about their jobs and experiences and then find training or similar places where you can gain skills that are directly related. In all cases, you are the driver of the situation. It is time for you to find the motivation to further your knowledge base, which will add to your career Æ value.

Finding the motivation to do something is a challenge for most people. You have most likely tried to increase your willpower to change an aspect of your life. How did that work? If you are like me, it did not work out well. Why? **Because we are focusing on the wrong thing.** The best way to change is for us to find ways to decrease the **resistance** we meet to get to our goals. These are the barriers that make it difficult to change our ways and to form better habits.

For example, I know that I must eat better and exercise so that my body does not work so hard to stay alive. My weight is about 15% higher than it should be, but why can't I just say, "I am going to lose weight," and then make it happen? While that sounds good, I find myself at vulnerable times of the day when it falls apart, and I fall back into the habits that keep the weight right where it is.

To be successful in achieving my goals, I do not rely on my willpower any longer, but work to remove the barriers that keep me from getting there. If I like to eat or drink specific items that are not helping me reach my goal, then instead of having them in the house and summoning up my "willpower" to not consume them, it is more effective for me not to have them in the house at all. By removing the barrier, I cannot eat or drink the items if they are not in my presence,

I do not have to rely on my willpower to keep me from not meeting my goals.

I found a new technique, one based on managing time, which works well for me, and I feel I now have more control. Instead of focusing on calories consumed and the types of food, I have set the goal of only eating for a 12-hour period during the day, providing my body with at least 12 hours each day in which it is not processing calories. I have found that I can manage that task more easily. An added benefit is that I do not snack in the evening any longer since it falls outside of my allotted time. You can create ways that work to motivate you to reach your goals.

In his book, *Drive: The Surprising Truth About What Motivates Us*[45], Dan Pink asserts that the secret to being a high performer at work, school, and home lies in our deep-seated, human need to direct the outcome of our own lives. As a result of his extensive research, he helps the reader understand the difference between "extrinsic" and "intrinsic" motivation, and how knowing the differences can bring you more satisfaction in what you do.

Extrinsic motivation is often described as a "carrot-and-stick" approach where some external stimulus is causing you to behave a particular way. The reward or consequences of your actions are directly related to you taking action, or avoiding an activity, and the external provider controls the situation. One of the largest faults with this type of motivation is that upon removing the reward or consequences, you will typically return to your previous behavior.

An example I often use in workshops is to imagine a donkey that you need to move. Placing a carrot on a stick and dangling it in front of the donkey will get the donkey to move forward, hoping he will reach the carrot and earn his reward.

As long as the carrot is there, the donkey will move. Remove the carrot from his sight, and he will stop, as the incentive to chase the reward is gone.

In the course of the donkey moving forward, he will be so focused on the carrot that he could walk right over a cliff without noticing. In this case, the donkey's behavior may seem odd, but not when you consider that if the donkey wanted that carrot and was putting all of his efforts into that activity, other activities become less important and he stops focusing on them.

I am sure you have witnessed this around you, and perhaps have done it yourself, when you are so focused on a task or assignment that you lose track of some other necessary activities or people in your life. Now is an excellent time to review the list of life priorities that I shared in Chapter 3 and the expectation that if over time your list does not rebalance in that order, the other areas of your life will face the consequences. Just as with extrinsic motivators, don't lose focus on everything around you for long periods of time if you want to maintain control of your career.

Pink also claims that intrinsic motivation is based on three aspects of our lives:

- Autonomy
- Mastery
- Purpose

Autonomy describes your inner drive to do well. When you are given autonomy over a situation, you are allowed to use your judgment and experience to make a decision. This puts you in control of the direction you take and allows you to feel the satisfaction when it works well. Think about the last time you had this happen in your life, no matter how small or if it happened at work, at home or in your community. That deep sense of pride that you felt is because you had the autonomy to "take it and run" to get things done.

This is one of the area's most of us lack in our jobs. While we may have the experience and knowledge, it is up to the leaders to provide the autonomy for us to be our best. If the leaders are not aware of how to manage this or lack the self-confidence to let the team be in control of the work, then it is difficult to feel that you have power over the direction of the project and you become less engaged in the process. Later sections of this book will help you find ways to increase your autonomy.

To describe why mastery is so essential, I ask you to think of a person you consider to be the "go-to" person for any topic. There should be a few people who come to mind for different areas of your work life. What makes these people the "experts"? How did they get to that point?

The answer lies in their ability to become a master of that topic. It can be a work process, legal compliance issue or anything for which the person has gathered enough experience and knowledge that people will turn to them for information or advice. While some people purposely focused on becoming that expert, others evolved into that role through time they spent in a position. Some of them will even tell you that they are not an expert, but merely the only one around that has ever done the task.

No matter how the "go-to" person arrived at that point, it is important for you to find a way to become a master of a topic or process. Invest the time to learn new skills and work with people until you become the one who people turn to for advice. As you do this, do not fall into the trap of hoarding knowledge to maintain the "expert" title, as, from my decades of experience, it is the expert who teaches people what she knows that becomes the trusted advisor. Your aim of mastery is to become a trusted advisor and not just the "expert."

The last aspect of intrinsic motivation has to do with purpose. In their book, *Passion and Purpose*[46], authors John Coleman, Daniel Gulati, and W. O. Segovia describe how searching for a purpose is the wrong question. Instead, we should be looking to incorporate purpose into everything we do. They assert that we can find meaning in what we do if we understand that purpose is based on the context of the situation, which means that there is no one single purpose for our work and that it evolves and changes over time.

The secret to finding purpose in your career is to determine how you put passion into what you do, not take it out. This means you have to put your entire self into your work and career, not just the person who shows up for a 9-5 shift. You have to let go of the fear of not being good enough or missing a target at times. Failure is part of the journey to building purpose. Embrace that understanding and your goal will become a significant driver of your career success.

As we have learned, extrinsic motivation is not the best choice for long-term success. While there are times that being rewarded for a particular activity is beneficial for a short-term gain, your career success is better served through a deeper understanding of how you can create autonomy, mastery, and purpose in your career.

Your motivation is contagious because people who have more enthusiasm and willingness to learn will persist and persevere and become role models to others around them. You need to change your behavior to affect change and avoid burnout. Develop the way to become motivated to be a better you and your career will blossom.

The time to begin is now. Think of the last time that you were ready to change jobs, faced a layoff or were fired. At that moment, you suddenly became more aware of the skills you lacked or the experiences that you did not have that would have helped you move into the next job. Find the motivation today to develop your plan and avoid that happening to you again.

The most challenging situations in my career appeared when we faced a crisis that required a small group of us to work closely together. In the cases where I had built relationships with people beforehand, we were able to more easily rely on the trust in each other that we had created, and the transparency allowed us to work effectively towards a solution. We did not worry about each other's motives.

But in the cases where I had not fully developed the working relationships, or worse, had experiences with another person that degraded trust between us, it was challenging to work towards a solution. Each time one of us would recommend an action, we found ourselves over-processing the activity to determine if the other person was trying to position himself for reasons other than solving the crisis. By not focusing on building a foundation of trust when the times are good, we were not able to fully leverage our capabilities and develop a practical solution to the challenge. And like focusing on improving your skills only when you have to react to a situation, trying to build the relationship during the time of crisis is complicated and fraught with risk.

Think like a fresh graduate out of school who is eager, inquisitive, and ready to take on the world. Your years of experience have worn you down. You don't ask as many questions any longer. You have become a bit complacent in your job and possibly even a little cynical. It is up to you to change this attitude to one where you are proactive and engaged, actively pursuing the goals you want to reach and the achievements that you desire. The only thing holding you back from this is you.

Whatever you do, just start with an action. Don't wait to create the perfect master plan. Pick one activity and get started today. Think of it this way; it is easier to edit something on your list than it is to create a list, so develop a list to get started and take it from there. Let's start the journey together.

Chapter Debrief

- Remove obstacles from your journey as you understand, develop and promote your entire Æ value

- Choose intrinsic motivators to focus on, like autonomy, mastery and purpose

- Don't search for a purpose, but use your passion to incorporate purpose into everything that you do

Your Turn

1. Make a list of the three things you need to accomplish to be considered the "go-to" person in your company.

2. Write one sentence that describes the last time you put an intense amount of passion into an activity.

MOVE YOUR Æ

Part 3

Show Your Career Value

16

Harness the Power of Change

> There are no shortcuts to any place worth going.
>
> — Beverly Sills

At this point in the book, you have discovered why it is essential to know your career value so that you can continue moving ahead and not be left behind. I also shared with you an entire section of the book where you learned techniques to grow your career value. It is now time to focus on promoting your excellent career value.

There are three steps to build the foundation from which you can announce to the world the value you add while navigating your career journey. No matter if you are learning a new skill, living an experience or earning a credential, the three parts of the process are the same:

- Awareness
- Learning
- Practice

I call this the "ALP" foundation, an acronym of the first letter of each word. The upcoming three chapters are each devoted to a step in this process. To most effectively show your career value, you have to be able to compare your career value to the career values of other people with whom you work or compete in the job marketplace. As I mentioned previously, two people can have a similar value, but the composition of what determines worth can be very different. By following this process, you create an understanding of the anatomy of your value to compare it to the structure of other people who developed a similar value.

Just like ascending the mighty mountains called the Alps, you are embarking on a challenging set of tasks that will force you to evaluate your strengths, learn more about your limits and cause you to adapt to the changing conditions. To do this well, you first need a deep understanding of how to harness the power of change.

There is a well-adopted model of change management called ADKAR®[47] that was created by Prosci founder Jeff Hiatt. In this model, Hiatt used his research to identify five outcomes that an individual must achieve for change to be successful. Let's take a look at each of them.

Awareness

Awareness is your understanding of the need to take action. You recognize the need to focus on your career to keep it on track. By paying attention more closely to what you do each day and documenting this information, you develop a stronger assessment of what you have accomplished, which gives you a jumping off point from which you will launch the changes.

Desire

Being aware of the need for change is not enough. Your motivation to make that change drives the process. Changes to your career involve your aspirations to reach higher, do more and be recognized for your accomplishments. Your passion to improve your current situation is the fuel for change.

Knowledge

Of the five outcomes, this one is the most concrete. Given any topic, you can easily find ways to gain experience, especially with the internet. The challenge with this step is determining how to allocate your time and money to identify the best sources of the knowledge, including the experts you turn to for the lessons. To be most effective, include methods to collaborate with other people while building your proficiency, as we can learn so much from each other.

Ability

This is your capacity to put your knowledge into practice. Book-smart people know information, but engaged practitioners put it into action. This outcome is where you press down on the accelerator to move. There are times in which you will wonder why you are taking on this change and that is normal. Use what you learned in the previous steps to remain focused on why this change needs to happen and tap into your creativity and aptitude to get it done.

Reinforcement

You need support to keep you from reverting to the original position. It can get tough at times of change, and it might appear easier to just go back to doing something the way you always have done it. But don't give up. Create a support network of advocates and allies who understand the need for the change and turn to them as needed. Everyone faces change in their lives. Just as they are available to you when you need their support, you will be there when they need your help.

Learn this change-management model and apply it each time you face change. If you are a leader, it is especially important that you understand how to leverage this model so that your teams tackle change effectively. I have used this plan for many years, and it has helped me better understand how to promote my abilities by getting people to buy into my ideas for change. You now have the tools to achieve similar success.

Chapter Debrief

- Understand and accept that while change may not be easy, it is a necessary step in growing your Æ

- Use the ADKAR® model as the foundation for change

- Book-smart people know information, but engaged practitioners put it into action

Your Turn

1. Create a list of three changes that you dealt with over the past six months.

2. Using your list from above, review and document how the five outcomes from the ADKAR model would have helped you get through the change more easily.

17

Awareness

Raise your awareness and share your
uniqueness to the world.

— Amit Ray

If you want to develop a new skill, the first step is to build an awareness of the ability, including your level of proficiency. You need to determine what defines the skill, how it is measured and what opportunities are available for you to become proficient. You can then develop a chart to rate your level of ability for each attribute. Understanding your levels of competence in that skill is an essential part of building your awareness.

As you saw in the ADKAR® model, awareness was the first step. It is essential to have a knowledge of the change and why the change is happening. As you work to promote your ever-changing career Æ, you need to start by recognizing the skill you want to develop. The more awareness you have, the more autonomy you will have over your career.

The internet is a great resource that you can use to start your research. Find out if there is a group of people who share the skill or if there is an association or other organization to which people with this ability belong. Their websites will contain a lot of information about what it takes to develop that skill. Review the LinkedIn sites of professionals who have this skill to learn more about their backgrounds, including the jobs they have had, the people they follow and interests that they indicate on their profile. Read their recent posts and articles to discover related people, then review their profiles.

One of the best tools you can develop is that of discovery. Learn to be an explorer or scientist who is trying to uncover how something works and why. By using these methods, you will find associated information that would have been difficult to find directly. It is the indirect information that you discover that will separate you from others who are also trying to develop this new skill.

As you research and build your awareness, you are likely to develop anxiety about not being able to catch up to some of the people you are finding in your research. They are going to appear to have developed a level of skill that is so far ahead of you that you are likely to feel overwhelmed. But there is a reason that you should not over-generalize that you cannot ever make a change or that you will always be behind them. That reason is that everyone started somewhere.

Keep in mind that you are seeing some of these people after they have spent years, possibly even decades, building their awareness, learning and practicing their trade. To keep you on a similar track, remove the absolutes from your vocabulary, like "always" and "never." Seek the balance between what is possible today and achievable in the future after you develop and follow many incremental steps.

It is crucial for you to build resiliency by having the awareness needed to concentrate and focus on your strengths. Accept your shortcomings, but do not be overly critical of yourself because of them. As long as the weaknesses are not hindering your development or taking away from your value, they will not have a significant impact on your ability to learn and grow. Your attitude and resiliency are the keys to success.

Should you get out or stay in your comfort zone? I know I am going to get some odd looks for this one, but it is okay to stay in your comfort zone, sometimes. That is right. You cannot always be pushing farther and faster. Like a high-performance athlete, you have to have cycles of strengthening and conditioning, followed by periods of rest.

The same is true for your career. Most of the time, you should be striving to improve and stretch your comfort zone. But it is also important for you to be aware that it is okay to stay in your comfort zone once in a while. You worked hard to get where you are, so enjoy the zone you have built. Do not let the Type A personalities make you feel guilty for spending time in your zone. As long as you have a plan that you are following and working towards, there is a lot to be said for a period of rest and reflection while you bask in the rewards of your current comfort zone.

When it is time to get out of your comfort zone, relationships are vital to gaining traction on your out-of-comfort-zone expedition. When you take this step, you open the opportunity to learn more things about yourself and other topics. To survive, you must develop agility that you did not need as much in your comfort zone.

Your agility gives you the ability to recognize when to continue down the learning road you intended to travel and when to veer off the path when it is not taking you in the direction you want. The more you do this, the more comfortable being agile becomes. You learn, as I have, when to zig and when to zag. It is easy to stay in your comfort zone and difficult to move out of it. If it were easy, everyone would be doing it. By stepping out of your comfort zone, you increase your value and move your Æ.

Simon Sinek often mentions in his talks about how he uncovered his "golden circle[48]" concept that "what" you do is less important than "why" you do it. Through this process, he uncovered that his "why" is to help everyone want to get up in the morning and go to the place where they go because they know and appreciate why they are doing it. You can also discover why you do what you do with a little thought.

For instance, how did you get the current job? Did you find it because someone you know works there? Was it because you like what the company does, such as its purpose? Perhaps it is because it is the company in your area that had a job opening that you could handle and you needed to earn money. Yes, it may be that simple. In any case, you need to build the awareness of "why" you do what you do before you can embark on the rest of your career journey. I want to make sure you don't wake up one day and say, "Where am I?"

As I approached the grand age of ½ century (I don't mind saying the number of years, but I know that it bothers a few of you), I began to reflect on my career journey so far. I went all the way back to my childhood so that I could gain the perspective of my foundation years to understand better how I got to my current way station on the journey.

Our youngest child was about to leave for college, which left my wife and me as the proverbial "empty nesters." We were also celebrating our 25th wedding anniversary. As I looked back, I realized that she and I had met when we were about 25 years old. This made me realize that we had two equal periods in our lives so far, one with and one without each other. I called them the first and second chapters in our lives.

During our first chapter, we both grew up, were educated, and ventured out into the world as adults. Then we met, she somehow put up with me and wanted to marry me, so we were married, had two children, created our home and embarked on our careers. That was the second chapter, and it was a lot of fun. It is a good thing we were younger and sprier in those days, as it consumed a lot of our energy.

Now we were entering what we call the third chapter. I witnessed many people around us that did not pay attention to this transition. They simply kept doing what they had been doing by getting up each day, going to work, vacationing a few times a year and waiting for retirement. That was not sitting well with me. My wife and I discussed it, and we decided we were going to be the drivers in our third chapter and not just go along for the ride. We have plenty of energy left, and while we enjoy working to earn career achievements and make money, that was not going to be our purpose for the next 25 years. We are in control, so look out world!

So I ask you, "Where are you on your journey?" Have you developed enough awareness to understand where you came from, where you are and more importantly, where you are going? I am asking you to do just that. Take a few minutes each day for the next two weeks and think about it. Jot down some notes and put them into your Memory Jar. It doesn't have to be complete sentences, but quick notes on your journey. If you have a partner, share the thoughts with him or her. Ask that person the same questions and see what you have in common. For you to take on the next phases of continuous learning and practice, you need to have a solid awareness of who you are.

For me, I am a teacher at heart. I have always received a tremendous amount of satisfaction when I help others learn. What many don't realize is that no matter the teaching situation, I learn something myself. While I understand that I am imparting knowledge, it is how the message is received, and the action the person takes that teaches me a little about that person and helps me adjust my methods for future sessions.

That is why I spent the hundreds of hours compiling the information, writing this book and developing the companion resources. I love to help people become more aware, create stronger capabilities and find success. I thank you for reading this book and giving me satisfaction for my efforts.

Chapter Debrief

-   As you move along in your career, it is okay to stay in your comfort zone at times to enjoy the fruits of your labor, but have a plan to keep improving at a point in the near future

-   Use the profiles of professionals on LinkedIn to discover attributes about a profession you are targeting

-   Understand where you came from, where you are, and where you are going in your career journey

Your Turn

1. Break up your life into "chapters," list them, and then write three sentences for each chapter to tell the story.

2. List three areas of your career where you are in a comfort zone. For each zone, set a date within six months by which you will focus on expanding out.

MOVE YOUR Æ

18

Learning

Life is school.
If you don't learn every day, life is passing
you by, and you are missing opportunities.
— Chris Williams

When was the last time you learned something? It is not as long ago as you think. In fact, if you read a story on an online news site, scanned an article on LinkedIn or listened to a podcast, you learned something. You probably even learned about recent events from a conversation you had with a coworker today. You are going to have to face the fact that you learn every day. It is what you do with this new knowledge that will impact your career.

As I indicated at the beginning of the book with the story about my daughter and the fire hydrant on our street, it is vital for you to know how to filter out the irrelevant new bits of information you learn each day. But be careful, as what you believe to be immaterial today or for a particular situation could be a piece of information you need to make a decision at a later time.

Your enthusiasm to learn affects how much you can learn. I am not saying that you need to be "rah-rah" about every learning situation, but that you should face each day, no matter how tired you are, with the attitude that you will learn something today. And as you have gathered from the topics in this book, you then need to document what you learned.

A critical factor that has a direct impact on your career is the willingness to learn. Above all else in your career development, you have to be willing and able to take on new challenges as you learn. This concept is called your "learnability," and you have to set this as a higher priority over earning credentials, as it is what hiring managers are now focusing on to determine if you will be a good fit with their organization.

The ManpowerGroup has a succinct definition of learnability:

The desire and ability to quickly grow and adapt one's skill set to remain employable throughout their working life.[49]

They even created a metric to quantify a person's learnability into a Learnability Quotient (LQ)[50].

Even if you do not know your LQ, it is crucial for you to understand the underlying assumptions of it to stay relevant to and succeed in your career. Here is a breakdown of the learnability definition:

Desire

You have to want to improve. No one but you will provide the motivation to learn. It is time to rekindle your passion for growing toward becoming a better you.

Ability

Do not short-change your ability to learn. Think about how much you have learned since you were a child. You have a large capacity to learn, even as an adult. You simply have to be reminded why it is important.

Quickly Grow and Adapt

As you have seen in your life, technology has increased the speed at which we do everything, including how quickly you must adjust to new conditions. Do not let complacency creep into your comfort zone and keep you from venturing out of that safe space to grow.

For a company, employee training is essential for retention and performance. That is why you see that the top companies to work for always have strong "Learning and Development" groups within their organization. These teams are focused on helping the workers in their personal and professional development by creating programs that help the employees understand more about how they work and why they function the way that they do.

These programs are designed to help the employee grow, but they must also be aligned with the organizational goals to support increased business value, which means that they are mostly interested in your value to them, not your value to you. Taking advantage of these programs where you can is key to your success, but make sure you understand that you are responsible for your career development. Your ability to keep your job, and secure the career path that you want, should be high on your priority list.

A recent article in the *Harvard Business Review* describes the concept this way:

Higher career security is a function of employability, and that, in turn, depends on learnability.[51]

Here are three themes on which you can focus to expand your learnability:

Communication

Learning how to communicate begins with understanding how you learn. That sounds somewhat like the riddle about what came first, the chicken or the egg, but it is not. To be an effective communicator, you must understand how you perceive your world.

When I was earning my undergraduate degree in mathematics, I also enrolled in education courses so that I could be a math teacher when I left college to start my career. I had a course one semester that was taught by a well-respected education professional. He had many years of teaching experience, was a genial man, and showed me one of the most powerful lessons that still has a direct impact on my career today.

On one cold, snowy, Vermont day, he stood at the front of the classroom and asked each student to do something. He asked us to sit quietly for a moment and to picture an image of our mother's face in our minds. That was it. Just picture your mother's face.

I quickly imagined my mother's face with her deep brown eyes, her dark hair and her cheekbones that set high on her face. My mother did not wear makeup often, so I did not picture her wearing makeup. She did have cats that she loved, so I imagined her face as it would light up when she was caring for one of her babies (my sister and I were adults by this time).

The professor then asked us to do one more thing. Without making any sound, raise our hands if we pictured our mother's face in full color. At first, I was a bit baffled by his question. I typically view images in my head in full color, so I was not sure why he was asking this question. As I raised my hand, I looked around the room.

Only about half of the students in the room had raised their hands, which astonished me! The professor had performed this act many times before, so he just smiled as he watched our looks of amazement as we glanced around at each other, noticing the ones who had either raised their hands with us or had not.

He then made the statement that not everyone sees, imagines, thinks and learns as we do. As teachers, it was our responsibility to understand that we needed to be keenly aware that not only are our learning styles different from other people's learning styles but that how we learn is rooted in how we communicate through touch, sound, and sight. From his lesson, I learned that for me to communicate effectively with others, I need to understand better how they receive and process information since it is most likely very different from how I do it.

For your career, you need to understand how you communicate to be most effective at learning. If you are someone that learns more from a visual environment, then find opportunities that support this learning style. If you learn more when there are discussions, even debates, around topics, then find places where you can experience more auditory-style learning. Finally, if you learn best when you get to touch items, then a tactile-focused learning environment is best for you. There is no right answer, but there are better ways for you to learn through your communication style.

Persuasion

I am going to make a statement that violates one of my earlier rules of removing absolutes from your vocabulary.

**Every successful person
is skilled in the art and science of persuasion.**

Why am I bending my own rule and using the word "every?" Because it is true that you must work with other people to accomplish goals toward becoming successful. And to work effectively with other people, you have to be able to persuade them at times to follow your idea or lead. Your ability to sell an idea or negotiate conditions has a direct impact on your career success.

Learn to persuade more effectively by mastering these skills:

Know Your Audience

What you say and do does not matter. How others perceive and understand what you say and do is what matters. Understanding your audience allows you to craft your message so that they grasp it. You need to use vocabulary that is quickly recognized by them so that they spend more time on the content of your message than interpreting your words into a context that they understand.

Express Your Thoughts Clearly and Concisely

We have all witnessed situations where a person who is attempting to persuade us continues to say the same thing over and over. Brevity has always been preferred, but it is crucial in today's limited-attention world which is driven by messages that bombard us everywhere we go. Learn the art of quickly and concisely expressing your call to action for the audience.

The best place to start is called an "Elevator Speech," which is a 30-second snapshot of your idea that you can present to someone during an elevator ride. It is a great way to build the foundation of your concise message of persuasion. From there, add only the relevant items that will increase the awareness of your cause, but be blunt with yourself as you make this decision. Let 3-5 items that are necessary, into the discussion. Leave all other issues for follow-up discussions.

Be Genuine

For most people, this comes naturally. Some people have learned techniques to attempt to exhibit attributes that they believe make them appear genuine. Do not do that, as it is difficult to support this masquerade over time. Identify what drives you and write down the characteristics that accompany those attributes, which reveals your genuine self. Make sure that is who the world sees each day.

Tell a Story or Paint a Picture

There is a reason picture books are popular, even as you grow older in childhood. A great picture can convey a message more quickly than a set of words and our brains are built to process the image more quickly than a large paragraph. Think about how billboards and magazine covers are designed to draw your attention. Many of the techniques the publishers use are related to photographs and pictures.

To effectively persuade, tell a story that paints a picture in the minds of the audience. With a personal account, you achieve a higher level of engagement because it allows the humans in the audience to more quickly understand you, relate to you, and then listen to your message. I have learned through my extensive LinkedIn network that being slightly vulnerable in your story, where you may reveal a failure, can be a more powerful way to make a connection with other people. Try different methods to find out what works best for you.

Be Firm, But Not Pushy

As an entrepreneur, I can tell you that this is one of the most important aspects of being successful at persuasion. I have been knocked down many times after failures and told that my ideas would never work. Faced with those odds, it becomes more difficult to muster the courage to drive forward, but you have to continue to persevere.

Perseverance requires you to be firm in your pursuits and conversations with people, but not be overzealous to the point where you become annoying. When you are attempting to persuade someone to follow your idea, stay firm, but do not be obnoxious.

Smile Often

In this list of skills, this is by far the easiest, cheapest, and quickest one to develop. Just smile. You will be amazed at how powerful a smile is to people. To practice this, focus on moving your upper lip inward toward your top teeth, which will cause the ends of your mouth to curve upward. Practice in front of a mirror until you see how simple, subtle moves can make your lips form a smile.

One other way I have discovered that helps me keep a smile on my face throughout the day is to have some of my favorite songs in my head. As I hum sections of those songs, even quietly, my lips will form into a neutral or smiling position. By doing this, people will notice, and they will be more attracted to listen to your story.

You have so much more power to persuade than you believe, even at work. A *Harvard Business Review* article discusses how "...employees tend to assume that their influence is dependent upon their roles or titles — that if they lack official clout, they can't ask for anything.[52]" The author goes on to provide research that asserts that you have the power to persuade no matter which position you hold. It comes down to asking for what you want. Do not assume that you know the answer. Build a few, concise statements that focus on what you want and ask for it. People like to help other people, and your goal is to figure out how to get them to agree with you.

Critical Thinking

The third skill that is needed as you learn is critical thinking and is one of the most sought-after skills by employers today. The issue is that the term is used to cover a broad range of abilities. At its core, the ability to think critically means that you can analyze information objectively and make a reasoned judgment. The three key parts of this statement are:

- Analyze information
- Be objective
- Make a reasoned judgment

To be effective at analyzing data, you have to develop a system by which you will collect the data, store the data, and then retrieve the data to process the analysis. In the past, you would most likely have used a paper notebook to record the data then flip through the pages to develop your final analysis. Luckily for us, today's computers allow us to do this more efficiently, with a spreadsheet being a powerful tool that can store and analyze the data for us, including pivot tables, charts, and graphs from which we can create conclusions.

The next toughest aspect is to be objective. We bring a lot of our backgrounds and experiences into our decision-making abilities, which means that we tend to view data with a bias. If I grew up in a small town and you grew up in a big city, you and I look at a set of data related to city life from a different angle, as I do not know what it is like to live in a big city. It is not that I want to be biased against city life, but that my experience does not provide me with the best foundation to understand it. Be aware of, and try to correct for, any biases that your experience brings to the situation.

Finally, you use the information you have derived from the analysis of your data to come to a reasonable conclusion, and possibly take action. Keeping biases minimized during this stage is essential to make any judgments you express easier to explain and defend when other people review them. Use logic skills during this step to show how one piece of information links to another, which is how you came to your conclusion. There are times when you cannot provide a conclusion based on the information received, and that is okay. Be sure that you have shown the information to others in case they see patterns you do not.

Using the analysis of the data to make a decision is something that gets easier with practice. When you use data to make a decision, be sure that you have consulted with smart people who can help you decipher the data to make sure the information you are getting is valid and accurate. If the situation requires that you make a decision with the information, such as to launch a new product line or enter a new market, keep in mind that by not coming to any decision, you made a passive choice.

A few chapters back I discussed the difference between a choice and a decision and that decision typically affects your long-term career, so use all of your resources to validate the decision. The action plan you develop from this decision should have milestones at which you measure against a benchmark to make sure your choice is producing the results you need. This gives you the ability to make another decision based on the new data. In all cases, attempt to make the best decision you can at the time, given what you know.

It is easy to become overwhelmed with all of the learning opportunities available to you. Start with just one item. The sense of accomplishment you get from completing that one item will lead you to take on the next one. Learning in small increments allows you to compound the "learning interest" that you earn over time. Just like earning interest on your money, you magnify, boost, amplify, and expand your career value through learning something every day.

Chapter Debrief

- Your enthusiasm to learn affects your capacity to learn
- Hiring managers are looking for learnability, so be sure you have a strong understanding of how you learn
- Use the themes of communication, persuasion, and critical thinking as you expand your learnability

Your Turn

1. Make a list of the three ways you are going to smile more often.

2. Describe the last time that you used critical thinking (objectively analyzed information to make a reasoned judgment) in your job.

MOVE YOUR Æ

19

Practice

The greatest limitations you will ever face
will be those you place on yourself.

— Denis Waitley

At the beginning of the book, I discussed the framework
that James Clear describes in his article, "The 3 R's of Habit
Change." As you remember, those 3 R's are:

- Reminders
- Routines
- Rewards

For you to continuously practice growing your career
value, you need to form the habits that will allow you to
persist through the tough times. If you remember learning to
ride a bike, swim, read or write, you were not good at it the
first time. In fact, you were not good at it the second,
sixteenth or the fortieth time. But you kept practicing, and
your career is no different.

Use the framework of creating reminders so that each
week, you have a plan to allocate time to your career

development. If you use online resources to read and learn about specific topics, then set up a routine each day in which you avoid all other distractions and focus on that learning. And finally, document your progress using the tools from this book and the companion website (PaulCarneyWorks.com) so that you can create rewards when you achieve a milestone.

You have heard the notion that you need to plant a tree today so that you can have shade at a later time. But it goes beyond that, as the tree can also produce food for you or other animals, it can be a home for birds and could be furniture or firewood in the coming years. Taking one action today produces a wealth of returns for tomorrow. Stoke your career value each day through practice and like giving fuel and oxygen to a fire; it will burn brightly.

How should you allocate your precious time to practicing what you have learned? For you to be most effective at learning and practicing, one of the leaders in the talent development field, The Center for Creative Leadership, has research which supports that you should spend the majority of your practice time on experiences rather than classroom programs[53].

From this analysis, they recommend the following allocation of your time:

10% is spent in formal training, which includes workshops, online classes, tutorials and other structured learning sessions. People tend to allocate more time to these activities because they are the easiest to identify, schedule and then check off your list when completed. But industry research has shown that while this type of activity can introduce you to new skills and concepts, it is how you spend the other 90% of your time practicing the concepts that matter most.

20% of your practice time needs to come from interacting with people as you collaborate on projects and teams. It is during these interactions that you can try the concepts you learned. By accessing the other team member's experience and knowledge as you practice, you can more quickly determine the best way to apply what you have learned to multiple situations. At the same time, you allow others to see you in action, which is a great way to strengthen your network and promote your value.

70% of your time needs to be spent with on-the-job experiences in which you will best develop your skills. The hands-on adventures allow you to face the challenges associated with your learning in real-world, real-time situations where you can adapt as you practice. While you may be able to be a passive participant in a classroom or online setting, that is not an option in this case. The teamwork and partnerships you develop while working together and learning are key to strengthening your career value. And document what happens each day. You don't have to analyze what happened, just record it and place it in your Memory Jar.

To illustrate this point, think back to how you learned to ride a bike. Would it have been best if someone handed you a book that showed you how to get on the bike and turn the pedals while keeping your balance and steering? And even though the book would have covered how to stop using the brakes, would you fully understand the importance of the right amount of pressure on the brakes to stop smoothly versus a hard, jerky stop?

That would not be an effective way to learn how to ride a bike. While the instructions from someone about the moving parts of the bike and the concepts of balance, steering, and braking are helpful, it is not until you are on the bike and attempting to ride it that you understand how the three activities interact. And there is no better lesson than learning how much pressure is necessary on the brakes as you are heading rapidly toward that tree!

Likewise, your career development is best strengthened through practice in which you are an active participant. Regarding labor, we call it "rolling up your sleeves" or "getting your hands dirty." Using whatever phrase best suits you, develop your plan to practice each week. Keep track of the type of practice you are doing so that you allocate as much as you can to the hands-on, experiential activities for best use of your time.

In my career, I have used the CAR (Challenge - Activity - Result) method to develop the structure of my practice lessons.

- **Challenge**: This is the one thing I am taking on. There could be some sub-items that support this problem, but I try to focus on one issue that I am going to tackle. I suggest that you start by sticking with a challenge within your comfort zone of knowledge and expertise until you practice a few rounds. Once you have mastered this technique, you can take on more significant obstacles.

- **Activity**: For this item, I create a list of 3-7 activities that I will do to meet the challenge. The beginning items will focus on increasing my knowledge, usually through online studying, webinars or workshops. The rest of the list is set up to use the new experience directly in my life, both at work and in the community. Do not forget that you can practice learning new skills outside of work, such as volunteer work in the community.

-   **Result**: This is where I record the results of each activity as they relate to the challenge. Before I get started, I typically add a few items here to indicate what I might expect for results. Like the scientific method, I document a few expected results at the beginning to see if I come close to meeting them.

I have used another tool that helps me determine the tasks on which I am going to focus. It combines a look back at what I have done with a forward-looking perspective so that I can link previous activities to the next ones I do. This provides me with a reliable and consistent way to develop goals and process the results to pivot as needed and take action with the next steps.

The method is called **Start - Stop - Continue** and helps me group tasks into one of those buckets. You can set a time frame, like a quarter of a year or even a full year, then list the activities that fit each category.

-   **Start**: I list 1-3 activities that I want to start doing in the allotted time frame. These are things that I am not yet doing. Some ideas I have used in the past are to comment on more posts in social media, write more articles for my blog and to earn an industry certification.

-   **Stop**: This is typically a short list of 1-2 items that I am going to stop doing. These are activities that either do not add value to my current goals or hinder me from being effective. Some examples I have used in the past are to spend less time watching television shows and stop letting a past event in a previous job gnaw at me. That latter one, in particular, was difficult for me, as it was a situation over which I had little control but primarily affected my professional life. It took practice, but I have moved on.

- **Continue**: For this list, I review the documentation of things I have done over the past year and highlight the ones on which I want to continue focusing. Examples of these tasks are to reach out to at least five people each week if I have not talked with them in over six months and to make sure I keep that song in my head each morning so that I smile often.

As you use these techniques to determine your plan, track the changes you make. Since you cannot determine if you have improved when you do not measure your progress, how do you know the value you add to your job? Use simple techniques like Start - Stop - Continue to turn boring into efficiency. Take on tasks that others do not want. The stretch you feel as you reach for bigger goals will make you feel good about yourself.

Treat your career like you do with any relationship, whether it is starting a business, raising children, or finding a life partner. It is about your enthusiasm, energy and the resources you gather. Practice becoming a better you and your career will flourish. As you practice, keep in mind this thought:

**The future was yesterday's problem.
Today is your day.**

You are embarking on a journey, not aiming for a final destination, so keep focused on each step, one at a time, just as you would prepare for a long trip. Practice the route, gather the resources you will need along the trail, and then take off. The excitement of the trip will make you move quickly at the beginning, but then you find the right rhythm and you settle into the pace that will allow you to sustain the best level of exertion to keep moving.

If you take long sprints and are not heading in the direction that you want to go, you will end up farther away from a planned way station and have to backtrack. Keep the legs of your journey as small as possible, like short practice sprints, which not only allow you to have more periods of rest but also to reevaluate your current location and adjust your path as necessary.

Chapter Debrief

- Taking one action today produces a wealth of returns for tomorrow

- Stoke your career value each day through practice and like giving fuel and oxygen to a fire, it will burn brightly

- Use methods like 70/20/10, Challenge-Activity-Result, and Start-Stop-Continue to enhance the results of your practice

Your Turn

1. Pick one item that you are going to learn (review the previous "Your Turn" sections for ideas) and create a 70/20/10 plan.

2. Create at least two items for each of the Start-Stop-Continue steps.

20

Show Your Æ

> Great stories happen to those who can tell them.
>
> — Ira Glass

To begin the conversation about showing your career value, I am going to start with a philosophical question:

If a tree falls in the forest and no one is around to hear it, does it make a sound?

This question has many interpretations of its message based on what "sound" and "hear" mean. For our purposes, we ask that if an activity occurs and no one is there to observe it, does it matter? When put into context about your career, it would be something like this:

If you do great work and no one recognizes it, does it add value to your career?

What do you think? Is there still value added to your career if no one recognizes your contribution?

I agree that you can say, "Yes, I still added value," because what you did is now a part of your career story and can be used at a later time to show value. The magnitude of your contribution only matters within the current context, which is highly dependent on how thoroughly you document and promote.

You have learned techniques throughout the book on how to grow your value, and if you have not figured it out by now, you should also understand that you must consistently document your activities to identify your value. Differentiation of your value against the value of other people is key to winning the competition for jobs and promotions. Use the Æ tools to catalog your performance and strengths based on how you are different from others. Be excited that you have a head start since you are reading this book before they discover it.

Is there a right way to promote your value? No. But it is necessary for you to take action. How often do you get a performance review with your manager? How do you prepare for it? You hate it, don't you? Who can remember everything that you have accomplished over an extended period? How are you supposed to bring it all together when you are so busy doing your job.

If you are in a type of job where your work can be easily quantified, such as task-oriented, less complicated work that can be counted during a period of time, then your performance will be based on objective factors. It is easy for the leaders to add up your output and compare to others. What they tend to leave out are all of the other contributions you bring, like experience and knowledge that others may not have. Or your boss does not know how the work you did had a direct impact on business results. Without the proper understanding of this information, it is not calculated into the final evaluation of your performance.

If you are in a more complex job where analysis and decisions are based on credentials or professional knowledge, you are in a situation where your performance will be subjective, which means that there are typically no specific measurements of the input you provide to make decisions. In these cases, the organization may rely heavily on results, which can cause failures to be calculated as a negative value for you. Even though you documented what happened to cause the failure and the lessons you learned, you have to share this information in a positive way to support how it adds to your value. You need the ability to bring together everything you do into a well-documented, transparent standard, including the importance of failing, if you want to promote your total value to get the rewards you deserve.

Since everyone's Æ is unique, you have to provide the context of how you got to this point in your career, and you do that by telling your story. It is your story, and you are responsible for making it heard. Do not rely on your boss or company to provide the storyline and fill in the script. That is your responsibility.

When crafting your story to promote your value, review all of the items you have documented. Like any good story, you have to begin with the plot, which is what you want the other person to know. For your performance review, it is how the activities you completed added value to the team or company. Remember, do not just gather a list of activities you did and present them. That is not a story. And besides, they do not care about your activities, only how they helped the company make money, improve processes or meet the business goals.

Your story must be engaging, memorable and compelling to have the greatest effect.

Engaging

When promoting your career value, there are three parts to make your story engaging:

- **Problem**: Describe the issue that you were facing.
- **Action**: Provide details about the steps you took to investigate the root cause, then the plan you developed to tackle the challenge.
- **Results**: Discuss the specific effects that occurred as a result of your action plans. For this step, the more concrete and specific details you can provide, like before and after measurements, the more powerful your story will be.

Memorable

The goal of any story you tell is to share information and have people remember it. In your case, you want the recipient of your story, most likely a boss, to remember that you played a role in the success of the team or organization. The key to making an account memorable is to keep it simple to understand and if possible, use analogies.

An example of an analogy would be that if you are trying to describe how you solved a particular problem. You can state that instead of following the maze until you found the exit, you and your team moved yourself to a higher vantage point - above the labyrinth - so that you could see the paths more clearly and navigate down the correct path more quickly.

Compelling

Just as you are learning how to quantify your career value by using the Æ, your story must contain data that is pertinent to business results. Improving a process is only valuable if it helps save costs (time or money), or helps the company make more money. Talk about the successes you and your team had and how you played a role in meeting the goals. It is difficult to argue with success, so tell a story so compelling that they cannot refute the evidence.

When telling your story it is okay to be assertive, but do not cross the line and become aggressive or hostile. Be direct, honest, and decisive with your storyline. If your story lacks confidence, you will lose the trust of your reader. Recounting the exemplary value you add is not bragging. It is your time to shine, so focus on how to do it well.

Why you are successful matters as much as what you have accomplished. We are all a complex combination of the many parts that make up our lives, including identities in the professional and personal areas. Each identity is then a combination of relationships. In the personal world, it is your connection to family and friends. In the professional world, it is how you are perceived at work, on your team, and in your profession or occupation.

I am not only the combination of what I do at work and in my community, but also my interests and leisure activities. There are people with whom I connect during leisure activities that don't appear in other areas of my life. The few people who do appear in both provide a connection between the parts of my life. By making the connections between these people, I not only increase the value of my overall network, but I have people in the community who will tell stories of my ability to connect people, which helps to validate my efforts as I promote my value.

As you craft your story, be aware of your impact on others, primarily how they are perceiving and feeling about you. While you may say that you don't care what they think, you have to care to understand how they will treat you and ultimately support you when you need it. Think of every situation as one where you may need that person tomorrow to help you and change your behavior so that asking for that help tomorrow will be much easier and lead to a response of, "Sure, what can I do to help?"

One of the most powerful ways to promote your brand is to build trust and credibility by helping others. As you enrich their lives by doing something for them, you not only learn more about yourself, but you have people who will tell your story for you. As you have seen in life, the stories we tell about each other are more powerful and accepted than the ones we tell about ourselves. Helping others will give you a sense of pride and connection to your community, which will further strengthen your value. A strong value is more natural to express than a weak one.

I leave you with one final thought about promoting your career value. When someone is extracting value from a stock in the stock market, they need to buy low and sell high, with the ultimate act of value extraction being to sell. When you are attempting to capitalize on the investment in the growth of your career value, the value-extraction step is to tell your story.

Stock market: Sell, Sell, Sell
Your Career Market: Tell, Tell, Tell

Look carefully at how that statement is a concise, engaging, and memorable analogy to sell my point. You can also do it as you show your Æ to the world.

Chapter Debrief

- It is your story, and you are responsible for making it heard

- If your job involves complex analysis based on professional knowledge, you are judged on subjective items and failures can be calculated as negative value to your career unless you tell the story

- Make your stories engaging, memorable, and compelling

Your Turn

1. List three activities you accomplished in the past three months, then indicate for each of them if they saved the company money, made the company more money or improved a process.

2. Pick an achievement from the past six months and craft a short story (no more than 15-20 sentences) that is engaging, memorable, and compelling.

21

Your Next Steps

Congratulations! You made it to the end of the book.

Here are the steps I recommend that you follow at this point:

1. Visit the **PaulCarneyWorks.com** web site.

    - Download the templates and tools.

    - Sign up to use the online Æ tools to easily document and store your information in one place, including access to the **Æ Insight™** data engine to help you discover ways to grow your career value.

2. Review each of the "Your Turn" pages in Chapters 1-20.

    - Use your answers and insights as you complete the templates or upload your documents and information into the Æ Insight™ data engine.

3. Create an account (if you do not have one) on LinkedIn.

    - Even if you have used LinkedIn in the past, it has become a more powerful professional social media platform. It allows you to engage with and learn from people from many professions, backgrounds and locations around the world.

    - Follow people who influence professional engagement and encourage people like you to learn and grow. For an up-to-date list of influencers, visit the PaulCarneyWorks.com web site.

4. Make it a habit to document, develop and promote your career value.

   - **Commit to documenting what you do.** Until you do this, growing and showing your career value will be difficult and others will earn the promotions and get the jobs.

Want to know how to type the Æ on your keyboard?

Follow the instructions below to use the Æ in your emails, text messages, social media posts, or any document.

Mobile device (Android, iOS)	On the keyboard, click the shift key ⬆ to get the capital A showing, then press and hold the "A" key and select the Æ from the menu by sliding your finger
Windows	ALT-0198 Note: You have to type the 0198 on your numeric keypad
Mac	SHIFT-OPTION-' (that is the single apostrophe next to the return key)

Connect and stay in touch with me in all of the social media channels listed in the last pages of this book and on the web site. I look forward to being your advocate as you:

Dream Big, Get Stuff Done and Have Fun!

ACKNOWLEDGMENTS

To the person who made me set a date for my first book

At our first meeting in the fall of 2017, Steve Wilmer let me get half-way through lunch before he asked me to give him a date by which I would get my book to an editor. His challenge to me, along with his experience in writing books and launching a successful speaking, coaching and training business, were the inspiration I needed to bring it all together.

To my incredible editor

Susan Lewis of Proper Publishing made it easy for me to convert my thoughts, ideas and words into a cohesive message for a wide audience. She turns ordinary phrases and sentences into descriptive illustrations and I am forever grateful to have her on my team.

To the Friday Morning Coffee Klatch

There is a group of us that get together at the local coffee shop in downtown Pensacola each Friday morning to drink coffee, have discussions and solve the world's problems. One of them in particular, Steve Clopton, was the person who introduced me to Steve Wilmer. The rest of the crew: Jim Beran, Dennis Remesch, TJ Edwards, Kirk Waters, Josh Roth, Josh Flanders, Fenoy Butler and Dennis Schroeder have been an inspiration to me to finish the book and provide me friendship and support, especially when I needed it most.

To my friends and colleagues

So many people I work with have provided me support and guidance as I started this journey. There are more than I can name. To each of you I sincerely say, "Thank you."

I have built great relationships with people via LinkedIn who provide guidance and support. They include Chris Williams, Steve Crider, Victoria Tretis, Jannetje van Leeuwen, Catherine de la Poer, Mark Mayleben, Megan Ortega Tafolla, Karen Grosz, Kristin Sherry, Scott Berty, Bryan Wish, and Michael Spence.

Warren Gibbs, Carson Wilber, Cayes Delpeche, Tiffany Tolleson, and Brandon Gardiner provided support in many different ways. Finally, Linda Tilson and Elaine Pope were just a few of my beta readers who provided feedback and suggestions.

To my marketing team

I could not imagine how launching a book could happen without the intense support and feedback from Briana Snellgrove and the Social Icon team. They helped me make this book, web site and resources valuable for all of you.

To my mentors

CAPT Kevin Miller USN (Ret.) has been a tremendous asset as I navigated the book publishing process. Jim Harris offers his advice and inspiration, which have helped me to define what I want to do and the reasons to do it. Bob Larkin helps me learn about the field of HR, especially in a large, corporate setting.

MOVE YOUR Æ

Endnotes

1. https://www.ted.com/talks/barry_schwartz_on_the_par adox_of_choice

2. https://www.psychologytoday.com/blog/science-choice/201506/satisficing-vs-maximizing

3. https://www.ncbi.nlm.nih.gov/pmc/articles/PMC31816 81

4. https://www.psychologistworld.com/stress/fight-or-flight-response

5. https://en.wikipedia.org/wiki/Volatility,_uncertainty,_co mplexity_and_ambiguity

6. Ibid.

7. https://www.forbes.com/sites/work-in-progress/2012/11/26/the-surprising-poverty-of-too-many-choices/#2414c0a043c2

8. https://www.stephencovey.com/about/about.php

9. https://jamesclear.com/three-steps-habit-change

10. https://techcrunch.com/2017/11/05/jeff-bezos-guide-to-life/

11. Ibid.

12. https://www.entrepreneur.com/article/243218

13. https://twitter.com/IBMNews/status/92873733892612 0960

14. https://twitter.com/IBMNews/status/92837469083754 4960

15. http://www.yourdictionary.com/blue-collar

16. http://www.yourdictionary.com/white-collar

17. http://www.yourdictionary.com/potential

18. https://www.linkedin.com/in/evancarmichael/

19 https://www.ted.com/talks/simon_sinek_how_great_lea ders_inspire_action

20 Ibid.

21 https://www.linkedin.com/pulse/how-tackle-impostor-syndrome-new-year-melinda-gates/

22 http://www.yourdictionary.com/Value

23 http://sethgodin.typepad.com/seths_blog/2009/05/two -halves-of-the-value-fraction.html

24 https://en.wikipedia.org/wiki/%C3%86

25 http://fortune.com/best-companies/

26 http://www.yourdictionary.com/Value

27 https://en.wikipedia.org/wiki/Emotional_intelligence

28 http://csefel.vanderbilt.edu/resources/wwb/wwb23.ht ml

29 Hudson, N. W., & Chris Fraley, R. (2015). Volitional personality trait change: Can people choose to change their personality traits? Journal of Personality and Social Psychology, 109(3), 490-507. DOI: 10.1037/pspp0000021

30 https://tap.mhs.com/EQi20TheScience.aspx

31 https://www.druckerforum.org/blog/?p=860

32 https://www.amazon.com/Moneyball-Art-Winning-Unfair-Game/dp/0393324818

33 https://www.upwork.com/press/2017/10/17/freelanci ng-in-america-2017/

34 https://www.businessnewsdaily.com/10359-gig-economy-trends.html

35 http://govleaders.org/idp.htm

36 http://hrweb.mit.edu/performance-development/goal-setting-developmental-planning/smart-goals

37   Doran, G. T. (1981). "There's a S.M.A.R.T. way to write management's goals and objectives". Management Review. AMA FORUM. 70 (11): 35-36.

38   http://www.lorigreiner.com/mobile/hero-or-zero.html

39   https://www.ted.com/talks/shawn_achor_the_happy_secret_to_better_work

40   http://www.laurenchowe.com/

41   https://www.scientificamerican.com/article/a-self-improvement-secret-work-on-strengths/

42   https://www.amazon.com/Chasing-Stars-Talent-Portability-Performance/dp/0691154511

43   http://nationalsocialanxietycenter.com/2017/02/20/public-speaking-and-fear-of-brain-freezes/

44   https://www.statisticbrain.com/fear-phobia-statistics/

45   https://www.amazon.com/Drive-Surprising-Truth-About-Motivates/dp/1594484805

46   https://hbr.org/product/passion-and-purpose-stories-from-the-best-and-brig/an/10343-HBK-ENG

47   https://www.prosci.com/adkar/adkar-model

48   https://startwithwhy.com/simon-sinek/

49   http://manpowergroup.com/workforce-insights/expertise/learnability-quotient

50   https://www.learnabilityquotient.com/

51   https://hbr.org/2016/07/its-the-companys-job-to-help-employees-learn

52   https://hbr.org/2015/08/research-were-much-more-powerful-and-persuasive-than-we-know

53   https://www.ccl.org/articles/white-papers/putting-experience-center-talent-management/

Index

ABOUT THE AUTHOR

Paul is an accomplished business person whose career journey has spanned education, technology, finance and Human Resources. His agility as a business person allows him to learn how the specific function works and then build effective teams to do it better.

From the day he saw the first web browser in 1992, he set a goal to build an Internet-based company. He launched Ishtot, Inc. by 1997 and sold Baby Necessities™ gift baskets. Web tools were limited, so he had to build his own shopping cart and ordering system. His unique and highly-sought gift baskets were recognized in the *Wall Street Journal* as a "Best Value," and he sold the product line to a national retailer in 1999. He then helped build 2 more Internet-based companies.

Paul now devotes his time helping people with their careers. He combines what he learned while earning his M.B.A. and through building companies with his knowledge, experience and certifications in HR to help convert HR teams to trusted business advisors. As he does this, he has a keen awareness of how the employees can improve their careers.

He is a leader who guides people in their careers to:

Dream Big, Get Stuff Done and Have Fun!

Professional Credentials
- Master of Business Administration (M.B.A.)
- Senior Professional in Human Resources (SHPR)
- EQ-i 2.0® / EQ 360 Practitioner Certification
- MBTI® Step I and Step II Certified Practitioner
- Toastmasters
  - Competent Communicator (CC)
  - Competent Leader (CL)

Visit

PaulCarneyWorks.com

for tools, advice and videos for your career

Follow Paul on social media:

LinkedIn:	www.linkedin.com/in/PaulCarneyWorks
Twitter:	@PaulCarneyWorks
Facebook:	www.facebook.com/PaulCarneyWorks
Instagram:	@PaulCarneyWorks

Schedule Paul for
Speaking Engagements or Workshop Facilitation

PaulCarneyWorks.com

- Conferences and Keynotes
- Team Workshops and Leadership Summits
- Media Interviews (podcasts, radio, television)
- Business Networking and Career Events
- College and High School Career Events
- Community, Club and Chamber Events

Paul facilitates workshops based on concepts from this book and other career-related topics. He is available to come to your company or event and customize the workshop to your needs for both content and time. See examples on the web site.

Visit PaulCarneyWorks.com and let us know how we can help.